Teaching
for Equity

Elementary grades

Linda Crawford
Chip Wood

All net proceeds from the sale of *Teaching for Equity* support the work of The Origins Program, a nonprofit educational organization whose mission is to promote an equitable and humane multicultural society through quality education for all.

The stories in this book are all based on real events in classrooms. Names and many identifying characteristics of students and situations have been changed to protect the privacy of students.

World Wide Web sites mentioned as citations and/or sources for further information may have changed or terminated since this book was published.

ISBN: 978-0-938541-24-0

Library of Congress Control Number: 2014909631

Photography by John Goebel and Elizabeth Crawford
Cover and book design by Heidi Neilson

ヽレ゛ **ELEMENTARY**
ORIGINS
ⁿⁿ **DESIGNS**™

The Origins Program
3805 Grand Avenue South
Minneapolis, Minnesota 55409
800-543-8715
www.originsonline.org

23 22 21 20   5 4 3

To elementary school teachers and leaders
of the 21st Century

To the parents of the schoolchildren
of the 21st Century

To the children

—Chip Wood

To Amari

—Linda Crawford

Acknowledgments

The authors thank the readers, Josie Ahartz and Ruth Charney. Josie's compassion and skill in her work making school a positive place for students and their families invigorated our process as we developed the book. Ruth's enduring commitment to social justice as essential teaching practice in elementary classrooms, and her close reading and sage advice about how to best organize the book for the reader, inspired us.

Chip Wood

I would first like to send a special dedication and thanks to my granddaughter, Lily Aliyah, constant source of elementary school news, and then to thank the rest of my family that surrounds me with love: Reenie, Heather and Son, Isaiah, Belle Soleil, Jon, and Alex.

Many thanks to Terrance Kwame-Ross for inviting me into this work. Deep gratitude to my long-time friend and co-author, Linda Crawford, and friend and colleague, Jo Devlin. Special thanks to Elizabeth Crawford for her amazingly patient editorial guidance and deeply shared visionary commitment to the purpose of this book. Thanks, too, for the welcome and support from all my new colleagues at The Origins Program.

To Pamela Seigle and Lisa Sankowski at Courage & Renewal Northeast, thanks for your enduring friendship and partnership in our effort to create a bridge between theory and practice for the adult communities of schools, work that informs and is woven into the fabric of what is written here. I am similarly indebted to Deborah Leong and Elena Bedrova, authors and creators of *Tools of the Mind*, from whom I have learned so much; first through *Tools of the Mind* training and implementation in PreK and K programs and then through generous, on-going conversation with them and their colleagues Barb Wilder-Smith and Christine Jutres, who provided many resources and suggestions about the relevant application of Vygotskian practice in elementary classrooms. Christine's on-going engagement with me in her role as an elementary principal colleague and then as a *Tools* trainer has been invaluable.

Thanks to all my colleagues at Northeast Foundation for Children for so many years of shared dedication and commitment. Also, gratitude and respect to the teachers and administrators whose stories and inspirational teaching and leadership inform the pages of this book, especially educators and parents in the Gill-Montague Regional School District in Massachusetts, and the Regional Multi-Cultural Magnet School in Connecticut, especially those teachers who spent a school year exploring many of the practices in this book in their classrooms: Candy Bartsch, Hugh Birdsall, Sue Goldstein, Susan Hafler, Stefanie Hinman, Kelley Norcia and Director Paul Carolan.

Grateful appreciation to educator friends and mentors who have shared the call to teach and lead and listen over the years— Jonathan Ball, Terry Chadsey, Ruth Charney, Marlynn Clayton, James Comer, Paula Denton, Stephen N. Elliot, Jackie Haines, Sally Hare, Sam Intrator, Marcy Jackson, Rick Jackson, Roxann Kriete, Tom Likona, Jay Lord, Elizabeth Musgrave, Parker J. Palmer, Deb Porter, Sara Rimm-Kaufman, Ken Rocke, Maria Rodman, Maurice Sykes, Sharyn Wood.

Linda Crawford

One of the great pleasures in writing this book was working with teachers who tried out *Teaching for Equity* practices in their classrooms. Teachers at four very different schools chose to implement different strategies and then shared with us how the children responded, whether the strategy produced the desired effect, and how the educators felt about the experience. Sometimes they incorporated variations which became part of the practice. Sometimes they struggled, but always with the strong intention to persevere, to make it work. The best moments were when they reported the pleasure and growth the children experienced in an activity, or the pride of accomplishment. We are very grateful to these teachers, and to their administrators for encouraging them to participate in the pilot studies. I especially thank Kirsten Holmquist, Blair Jedinak, and Kalli Novak, primary teachers at New City School in Minneapolis, for their dedication to the project, and to the success of all their students, with no one left behind.

Jitendrapal Kundan, principal of New City School and my good friend, took an active part in all the explorations of *Teaching for Equity* practices, learning about them, encouraging teachers to explore them in their classrooms, and recognizing the results they accomplished.

I am grateful to Jessica Crawford, who opened her first-grade classroom to me at City of Lakes Waldorf School and showed me the power of learning basic skills such as reading, writing, and math through multiple modes—singing, playing instruments, gesturing, moving, and storytelling.

Other teachers who took interest in the project and tried a strategy in their classrooms or shared their practices with us were:

- Marcy Meyers, intermediate grades, New City School, Minneapolis, Minnesota
- Alissa Knutson and Ingrid Miera, primary grades, Fair Oaks Elementary School, Brooklyn Park, Minnesota
- Linda Hjelsted and Quennel Cooper, intermediate grades, Barack and Michelle Obama Elementary School, St. Paul, Minnesota

My partner in all these collaborations with teachers was Erin Klug. I am indeed grateful for the classroom experience she brings to our work together and her unfailing commitment to serve teachers well.

We are grateful to Dr. Terrance Kwame-Ross for providing us the opportunity to write *Teaching for Equity*. And because the task of writing a book is always a mountain to climb, I humbly thank our line editor, Jo Devlin, who astounds us with her ability to pull tight all our loping sentences so they say what we feel and think in a way that other educators can more easily hear.

Most amazing in the process of creating this book was the close collaborative spirit my two partners, co-author Chip Wood and editor Elizabeth Crawford, and I maintained throughout the process. I cannot imagine better partners in the effort to share strategies to help make school a place where all children are eager to learn and are successful.

Table of Contents

CHAPTER ONE

A Call to Teach for Equity

"Beyond the math, the reading, the science, the grammar, Elaine wanted her students to learn that they were part of a community. She wanted them to experience the sharing and the intimacy and the trust that can develop in a group. She wanted them to experience the joys of belonging, really belonging. She wanted them to understand that the learning they struggled so hard to achieve had a purpose, and the purpose was to help not just themselves, but also others." (Bob Katz, Elaine's Circle[1])

Welcome!

Teaching for Equity is for elementary teachers and teacher leaders, school administrators and specialists, teacher educators, school families, and school advocates who work to find or create a more just and equitable elementary school experience for students.

Teaching for Equity is about returning teaching and learning to the primary relationships between teacher and student, student and student, school and family.

Teaching for Equity speaks to what we can do individually and together to bend the arc of elementary education more toward the positive energy, spirit, creativity, and innate capacity of each child to gain mastery in essential social and academic skills and content. This is knowledge aimed at the fullest realization of their unfolding potential during their elementary years, as they begin to decide what is important to create in their lives—including nurturing their capacity to contribute to the good of the group.

Teaching for Equity is about approaches for eliminating the learning opportunity gap for children whose experience each year in elementary school often leaves them further and further behind their peers. All students ought to have the human and material resources they need so that equitable results are attainable.

We have written *Teaching for Equity* because we believe in you. We trust your intelligence, diligence, and compassion. We hold great hope that a new generation of diverse elementary teachers and leaders will join with veteran colleagues to move the agenda for equality of outcomes rapidly forward in the schools where you lead and teach.

Our experience

The authors of this book have witnessed the staggering costs and consequences of inequity for children and families over the last half-century, despite the best efforts of many. We have worked through eras of open education, pushed-down curriculum, back-to-basics instruction, developmentally-appropriate practices, whole-school reform initiatives, standards-based teaching, No Child Left Behind, data-driven instruction,[2] 21st Century skills, and now Common Core Standards and the dawn of national testing. We have provided professional development in constructivist education, social and emotional learning, arts integration, multicultural education, child development, reflective practice, democratic classroom management practices, and leadership.

We shared common purpose with thousands for a national education agenda that would level the educational playing field for all, and we have seen, instead, widening learning gaps that primarily impact students living in poverty and students of color.[3] Models of instruction feature external modes of assessments, standardized practice for standardized testing, and sorting, classifying, and isolating students, teachers, and schools by performance on standardized tests. All of these practices have not worked to close the so-called "achievement gap."

The U.S. Department of Education's Office for Civil Rights (OCR) Data Collection Report for the 2011-12 school year, released on March 21, 2014, scathingly defined the scale of the gap. The report offered "the first comprehensive look at civil rights data from every public school in the country in nearly 15 years.

"...This data collection shines a clear, unbiased light on places that are delivering on the promise of an equal education for every child and places where the largest gaps remain. In all, it is clear that the United States has a great distance to go to meet our goal of providing opportunities for every student to succeed, U.S. Secretary of Education Arne Duncan said."[4] (See endnotes for access to a report statement.)

Some say education is the civil rights issue of our time. Robert Moses, of the Algebra Project, says children are the civil rights issue of this century. "In the 21st Century," he said, "we need to include the children. They need to have a constitutional right to an education in this country."[5]

Education for equity

The Origins Program: Education for Equity, headquartered in Minneapolis, has been working since 1979 to provide teachers and schools around the country at the elementary and middle school levels with high quality professional development for classroom teaching focused on arts-infusion and multicultural approaches to learning how to read, write, understand and utilize scientific and mathematical thinking, how to work collaboratively, to participate democratically in sharing each other's strengths and resources; how to make school a rich part of life, not just a preparation for it.

The Origins Program's *Developmental Designs* approach helps secondary educators integrate academic, social, and emotional teaching and learning. This book introduces *Elementary Designs* approaches, created with and for elementary educators.

In every format of *Elementary Designs* professional development—workshops, publications, and consulting—the teacher assesses the needs of his or her students, designs the schedule for the day, and modifies it to suit individual students. Standards guide curriculum, of course; our goal is to help educators modify curriculum so that students can master the skills and content knowledge they need to grow from success to success. There is no autopilot in the cockpit of a classroom! As author and educator Salman Kahn writes, "You can standardize curricula, but you can't standardize learning."[6]

We affirm the teacher's professional right and obligation to teach with and for equity. Here we share our thinking about how your own intellectual and social capital can be shared most effectively with all of your students.

Teaching with Equity: Elementary requirements

To create an equitable foundation for learning, certain school and classroom conditions and experiences are necessary to meet the basic needs of students for *autonomy, competence, relationship, community,* and *play.* In this book, we explore seven strands of practice that grow equity in education:

- Personalized learning
- Personalizing whole-class learning
- Partnership
- Attuned student-teacher relationships
- Enhanced communication
- Teacher integrity
- Relational trust among adults, including student families

Provided these dynamic, interrelated social and cognitive pathways, children will grow in self-confidence; in self-regulation; in their capacity to learn for themselves, from their teacher, and from each other; and in their capacity to question. They will learn to work together productively, to care for each other, and to enjoy story, movement, music, poetry, drama, and image-making integrated with academic learning. They will learn how to listen—to be an audience, to learn the meaning of "me," "us," "we," and that how we are different creates our traditions and our cultures.

These practices, founded on decades of classroom experience and on ongoing research, address children's needs for autonomy, competence, relationship, community, and play. See Resources, page 164, for the underlying theories regarding the five needs addressed in *Elementary Designs* practices.

Throughout this book, we offer practical ways to link your standards, curriculum, lessons, instructional approaches, and your professional and personal growth to these equity-building practices.

Personalized Learning

Personalized learning provides students diverse ways to utilize their interests and strengths and gives teachers flexibility to adapt curriculum so each student can move from success to success.

Personalized learning, or *competency-based learning*, are summary phrases referring to variable structures for more autonomous academic instruction that allows "students to progress as they demonstrate mastery of academic content, regardless of time, place, or pace of learning.... These strategies include... project-based and community-based learning...among others. This type of learning leads to better student engagement because the content is relevant to each student and tailored to [his or her] unique needs. It also leads to better student outcomes because the pace of learning is customized to each student."[7] Students will be more able to competently and autonomously manage learning at the secondary level if they have practiced this approach with skillful guidance at the elementary level.

Everybody learns and grows

We hold that all students deserve personalized learning to build competence through cultural, developmental, and personal relevance. Using *Elementary Designs* practices, teachers scaffold learning for incremental success and proficiency for each student. Pacing for this requires matching tasks to a learner's ever growing stamina, autonomy, and persistence and knowing how to scaffold a child's emerging abilities and understandings. And we have long argued that the pace of learning in the elementary grades needs to take into account the pace of child development.[8] Curriculum pacing charts have to be used as tools for customizing the pace of skill and content mastery for each student, rather than as tools to evaluate a teacher's effectiveness in covering the same curriculum for all students in a predetermined time frame.

Newly acquired proficiency should be practiced repeatedly and successfully, in reasonable doses. Homework and class work should be apportioned so students daily experience their own success (not compared to others), which they can record and track in their own record books. In Chapter Three, we suggest ways to record and recognize student growth that can be shared with students in regular check-in conferences where success is celebrated and new goals are set. Students can share their growth through Yes! cards sent home to families frequently. The goal of incremental success is daily progress and increasing autonomy, confidence, and the capacity to reflect honestly on one's efforts.

Personalization and mandates

Personalized learning includes teaching children to share in planning some of their daily work, with options for activities and projects along with teacher-assigned work and small-group instruction. Teachers can use their mandated curriculum to structure independent, partner, and small-group instruction and follow-up assignments, just as they always have; personalization grows through the teacher's relationships with individual students and his/her observation and assessment of them as they work with others.

"It is the task of the teacher to guide children not just toward activity as an end in itself, but toward intelligent activity."[9] Planning and reflecting through writing, and/or verbally with a partner or with a teacher, personalize and consolidate learning continuously. They help a child realize his/her growing competency.

A decade ago, developmental psychologist and researcher Galina Zuckerman wrote: "Asking questions, formulating one's learning goal—such is the starting point of true learning, which has to begin no later than the first day of schooling. Only in this case will the majority of children, rather than only the elite group, become true learners."[10] Today we call such strategies 21st Century decision-making skills. We understand that teaching all students the autonomy necessary for such decision-making is necessary for educational equity.

In practice

Elementary Designs personalized learning practices:
- observing and assessing student activity and progress toward increased autonomy

- connecting and scaffolding tasks to student ability and interests
- rehearsing independent responsibility
- teaching children to plan and reflect on independent and partner work
- creating incremental success
- keeping growth records and sharing them with students and families
- facilitating check-in conferences with students

Enhanced Communication

A better balance of talking and listening and nonverbal communication between teacher and students enhances teacher assessment, attunement, motivation, and autonomy.

Educators must deliberately talk less and listen more in order to make room for children to talk more and listen to each other more about academic content, concepts, and skills. This is equally important for whole-class, small-group, and one-to-one communication. (It is also true in adult communication: teachers can listen more to students' families, administrators can listen more to teachers, etc.). We think of ourselves as good listeners, but curricular and behavioral demands seem to compel us to be thinking ahead as we listen, while simultaneously focusing on the one detail we want the student to understand, sometimes missing what a student is asking or trying to tell us.

The connectedness we trying to establish is *attunement*. Attunement in the classroom develops in meaningful one-to-one relationships between teacher and students. While every relationship is different, attunement occurs when the student and teacher are able to "read" each other easily through what is spoken, and, more readily through non-verbal communication and feeling tone.[11]

It can be enormously helpful for us to tune in:

- to build attunement with students so we can tell that they know we know what's up for them in a given moment;

- to identify how students understand content and skills by listening to how they talk to each other about content or how to do something;
- to be able to see a response as well as hear it;
- to teach children that their ideas have intrinsic value and that the teacher values their ideas—this allows for diverse sources of knowledge in the classroom;
- to scaffold student learning effectively.

Elementary teachers use scaffolding to plan incremental success and eventual independent mastery of academic skills and concepts. This calls for ongoing positive verbal engagement with students, as well as nonverbal communication such as written notes, sign cards, facial expressions, eye contact, and hand signals. Authentic positive feedback from the teacher for each student's and the whole group's academic industriousness is a key equity strategy.

The concept of scaffolding in education has its roots in the theory originally developed by developmental psychologist Lev Vygotsky, then explored through the research and application of many other cognitive scientists.[12]

The practice of scaffolding is observation and communication utilized by teachers to assess and support students' emerging autonomy, execution of skills, and grasp of concepts in what Vygotsky termed the *zone of proximal development* (ZPD), the place where children are able to accomplish tasks with assistance, but not yet autonomously. This assessment and support fosters student motivation and student-teacher attunement. "The teacher must be as active in the process as the child. While the child constructs the concept, the teacher is constructing the child's unfolding understanding through questions, probes, and actions. So the teacher strives to understand what the child understands."[13]

What the child understands

Striving to understand what the child understands is key for the teacher to adapt to and be open to each child's perspective, each child's culture and experience, to make each child's experience of school meaningful and enjoyable. Within such an affirmative environment, the teacher is much more able to foster each child's self-regulatory capacities of working memory, problem-solving, planning, organizing, and other executive functions.

A comprehensive study of "Tools of the Mind" school programs led by developmental psychologist Dr. Clancy Blair and behavioral social scientist Dr. Cybele Raver, both of New York University, hypothesized that "educational practices designed to support the development of executive functions will lead not only to higher academic achievement but will also be associated with beneficial change in measures of children's attention, working memory, inhibitory control, and stress response physiology."[14]

"Results from a cluster randomized controlled trial involving 29 schools, 79 classrooms, and 759 children indicated positive effects on working memory, reasoning ability, mathematics, the control of attention, and levels of salivary cortisol and alpha amylase. Results also demonstrated improvements in reading and vocabulary at the end of kindergarten that increased into the first grade. A number of effects were largest in high poverty schools, suggesting that a focus on executive functions and associated aspects of self-regulation in early education holds promise for closing the achievement gap."[15]

"Perhaps most important, a number of the effects we observed, including effects for salivary cortisol and alpha amylase, are specific to high-poverty schools. Recent research has highlighted the neurobiological and cognitive costs associated with exposure to poverty-related adversity. Our findings highlight that children in high-poverty schools demonstrate significant neurobiological and academic benefit when provided with an educational approach that provides scaffolded support for executive functions and self-regulation."[16]

In practice

Elementary Designs communication approaches:
- reduce teacher talk and increase teacher listening;
- refocus student listening to peer ideas as well as to the teacher;

- acquire scaffolding language and nonverbal strategies;
- enhance positive, appreciative feedback about growth;
- increase opportunities for peer audience;
- diversify communication to include visual, kinesthetic, rhythmic, and other modes.

Partnerships

Structured student partnerships nurture executive functions, especially working memory, decision-making, and self-regulatory interaction, as do partnerships among adults.

The pathway to equity is best traveled in two's. Critical learning patterns and habits are more firmly established and reinforced in academic partnerships than in isolation.

In American elementary schools, academic content is usually taught through whole-class lessons, teacher-led small instructional groups, or one-to-one by teachers. In each of these settings, content is transmitted mainly through verbal exchange between the teacher and students. Sometimes partners do a quick turn-and-talk activity to share opinions or understandings, and sometimes students work cooperatively in small groups or with partners on activities and projects to demonstrate their understanding of content. Frameworks for completing such work often help guide the students' as well as the teacher's assessment of learning and effort.

Partnerships for academic and social learning

Elementary Designs practices strengthen the effectiveness of these and other peer-to-peer learning experiences. Through coached partnerships, students learn a great deal about each of their classmates, about their interests and strengths, and about the academics that are hard or easy for each person. One-to-one, they increase their capacity to reflect, their self-awareness, and their ability to take the perspective of someone who may have a different idea about a story or game or mathematical solution, and they share about family and cultural traditions.

Partner responsibilities

In the first few weeks of school, the role and responsibilities of being a partner need to be discussed, role played, and rehearsed, and they need to be reviewed at certain times thereafter, for example after vacations and before field trips. Key recurring conversations for the class will be exploring the difference between partners and friends and the difference between times when you can choose a partner or you draw one randomly or the teacher chooses. A list of partnerships and partner responsibilities can be posted and updated through the year.

Partnerships can serve many functions: classroom jobs, reading and writing together, checking work, line partners for walking in the halls, and many more. In small groups for math games or word games, children can extend what they have learned from being a partner to take rotating responsibilities such as fact checking or judging a game of Four Square. Chapter Three discusses partnership approaches in detail.

Vygotsky's research

Our strong endorsement of partnerships is rooted in our direct experience with Vygotskian teaching approaches and research showing how children's capacity to understand each other's perspective can deepen as they are increasingly exposed to meaningful learning exchanges with partners who have different ideas or opinions. In one study where students were observed in first grade and again in fourth grade regularly exploring different solutions to mathematical questions with partners or in small groups, the changes over time revealed significant changes: as first graders, their thinking was focused solely on the subject, but by fourth grade, "the focus was both on the subject and the partner's interpretation of this subject. Such sophistication of the cognitive attitudes manifests the *decentration* of child thinking and emergence of a real learning dialogue between the interlocutors who do not always agree and yet understand or try to understand each other."[17]

Critical to many *Elementary Designs* approaches is Vygotsky's fundamental premise that "Every function of the child's cultural development appears twice: first, on the social level, and later on the individual level; first, between people (interpsychological), and then inside the child (intrapsychological). This applies equally to voluntary attention, to logical memory, and to the formation of concepts. All the higher functions originate as actual relations between human individuals."[18]

Thus, in elementary school, even the most basic routines are opportunities for children to use their developing self-regulatory skills in social interactions. The more they understand and experience how routines help the class have more time for projects and activities, the more the shared culture of the classroom will be internalized by each child.

Other-regulation and self-regulation

When the teacher shows that s/he values children's ideas, suggestions, and perspectives, their trust in the teacher increases, and their investment in their own and others' responsibilities to the classroom community increases. Without such developing attunement and trust between teacher and students, routines become drudgery, and the perceived value of learning slips.
In the following example we see how other-regulation leads to self-regulation in early elementary school.

"Being a tattletale is a symptom of the desire to regulate others. The tattler usually does not apply the rule to himself, but will be the first to shout out when someone else does wrong. The child wants to reaffirm the rule. For young children, the rule and the person who reinforces it are the same: 'I can take just one cookie because the teacher said so.' 'I am quiet because the teacher said to be quiet.' What children learn by using the rule to regulate others is the idea that the rule is abstract and exists apart from the person who enforces it. Once there is a rule, it can be applied in other situations. Then the child begins to internalize the rule or develop a standard. Instead of having to be reminded each time there are cookies that you take only one, the child now has a rule: 'When there are cookies or any food, you take only one at a time.' Likewise, the internalized rule about being quiet might be, 'I need to use a quieter voice when I am inside.' The idea that other-regulation precedes and prepares the way for self-regulation is not limited to social interactions but can also be applied to the regulation of cognitive processes."[19]

We have observed in our schools and programs the power of well-structured partnerships to deepen conceptual understanding, content comprehension, and competence when the social context of learning is well understood. We have seen how using student partnerships as a primary teaching methodology to facilitate and scaffold children's learning broadens the capacity of teachers to observe, assess, differentiate, and appreciate difference.

Chip learned a great deal from three years of first-hand experience with *Tools of the Mind,* an early childhood program for preschool and kindergarten based on Vygotskian principles, implemented in a district where he served as Director of Elementary Education. He saw remarkable growth in self-regulation and early literacy skills and in teacher practice. As an extension of this learning in PreK and K, he led teachers in the primary grades to discuss adapting some Tools practices in their classrooms. This work contributed to some of the initial conceptualization of *Elementary Designs* approaches.[20]

In practice

Elementary Designs approaches for student partnerships foster individual and collective competence in the classroom:

- teaching students through modeling, rehearsing, and activity what a partner is and does
- exploring ideas for use of partnerships in a particular setting
- varied partnerships—over time, everyone gets to be everyone else's partner
- school-wide partnerships across grade levels
- use of partnerships in before- and after-school programming

Personalizing Whole-class Learning

Opportunities for active, inclusive, creative learning together are essential to maximizing academic and social growth.

In the *Elementary Designs* approach, whole-class learning focuses *only* on learning that is appropriate to *every* child (this means no encounters with skills and information some are not ready to learn) and capitalizes on what learners can do together. Children learn responsibility by being given it incrementally—for taking care of their own materials, the classroom environment, and the way they treat each other. Daily activity is community in action: when the class gathers together, they experience the self-regulation and routines for give and take that characterize a healthy democracy. In these gatherings, students grow in their ability to learn from each other and to take care of self and other.

The power of community allows access to learning that is otherwise unavailable. Discussions are greatly enriched by multiple perspectives; differences of opinion stimulate hard thinking and the habit of producing evidence for your point of view; discussions that involve culture enrich everyone by sharing the diversity of the community. Lessons in observation or strengthening of memory or analysis of arguments and opinions create a classroom climate of rigorous thinking. Group decision-making mirrors the democratic process of shaping life in society. We are enriched intellectually, emotionally, and culturally when we come together.

Whole-class gatherings do not have to be fixed in class schedules; they can be used flexibly to respond to the needs of the community. In the circle, the focus of learning is on each other, on ideas, on problem-solving, and on having fun learning together. In addition to the content of the learning, a goal of whole-class gatherings is for students to learn how to respond to each other's ideas and not to dialogue only with the teacher. The teacher needs skills in whole-group facilitation, use of protocols, leading discussions, modeling and rehearsing expectations, and in reflecting on experiences and/or lessons.

In practice

Elementary Designs whole-class learning experiences nurture an inclusive classroom climate, facilitate transitions to reduce disruptions and promote autonomy, and introduce ways to respond to diverse needs by:

- Targeting curriculum that is best learned together, such as:
  - read-alouds
  - discussion of literature
  - discussion of content and form in other genres
  - discussion of current events
  - learning about historical events
  - science demonstrations
  - vocabulary development
- Gathering for specific purposes:
  - planning field trips, celebrations, service
  - connecting and learning in the first circle of the day
  - playing to build community and skills
  - cultural conversations to build understanding and reduce bias
  - sharing creative expressions
  - developing cognitive skills
  - building mindsets that support learning
  - being an audience for each other's ideas and work
- Developing climate and capacity for high participation with all voices heard
- Learning how to expedite transitions with mediators and nonverbal positive reinforcement
- Engaging and motivating learning at the beginning of the day
- Empowering student leaders and partners in room responsibilities and transitions
- Teacher strategies for classroom management:
  - caring, mutual attention
  - knowing and acknowledging students' positive attributes
  - changing negative labels to strengths
  - engaging and empowering students

- ideas for physical breaks, stress reduction, and self-care exercises
- personalized strategies for helping students get back on track

Teacher Integrity

Attention to self-knowledge and self-care in the adult community strengthens professional interactions and teaching capacity.

You were drawn to teach for a reason. You have invested in college and perhaps graduate education and have acquired experience. You are intellectually capable and have developed strength or specialization in at least one content area. You love being with your students. At the same time, you may feel stress, if not outright disempowerment, trying to meet all the mandated expectations from the federal and state governments and your district while still holding onto time to create a daily experience for children that meets *your* standards. Perhaps you wish you had more time to be with colleagues to plan or share. You may stay late and/or take a lot of work home, do school work on weekends, and have trouble balancing your personal life with your professional responsibilities. If you are a school leader, these observations likely apply to you as well.

We can only be as good for our students and their families as we are to ourselves and our families. We are aware that many of our students and their families experience severe inequities that cause overwhelming daily stress. We see how this impacts learning on a daily basis. We want our classrooms and schools to be places that provide relief from that stress, not add to it. Yet, as educator Parker J. Palmer writes, "We can be peacemakers in our small part of the world only when we are at peace within ourselves."[21]

The University of Toronto's Jim Cummins, professor of Curriculum, Teaching, and Learning and an authority on bilingual education and second language acquisition, points the way for teachers to begin to take charge of teaching for equity:

"Despite the pressures that are being applied to exclude critical literacy and student experience from classroom instruction, we always have at least some degree of freedom in how we interact with students, how we connect with their cultural experiences and language talents, how we involve parents in their children's learning, how we adapt content to link with students' prior knowledge, and in the level of cognitive engagement we try to evoke through our instruction. Alternative modes of assessment (such as portfolio assessment) can also present a counter-discourse to the inaccurate and misleading account of student progress and effort often reflected in standardized test scores. In articulating our choices, both individually and collectively, we rediscover our own identities as educators and also become aware of the identity options that our instruction opens up (or shuts down) for our students."[22]

In practice

Elementary Designs approaches to generating well-being and positive action among adults (most experienced in workshops):

- mindfulness and stress-reduction strategies
- expanded capacity for listening, observing, and being in the present moment
- professional time management skills
- reflection strategies for the workplace and the classroom
- self-directed implementation of *Elementary Designs* practices

Relational Trust among Adults

Reciprocal, culturally-conscious, positive relationships among colleagues and between teachers and families positively influence student success.

Teaching for equity requires trust and mutual engagement among all adults who influence the education of students both inside and outside school. In 2002, a research study written by a team of sociologists and urban education experts found groundbreaking evidence regarding the role *relational trust* plays in improving schools.[23] In *Trust in Schools: A Core Resource for Improvement*, Anthony S. Bryk, Barbara Schneider, and colleagues reported on three years of research in twelve elementary schools involved in school-reform initiatives in Chicago. Their study found that "elementary school communities characterized by high relational trust were much more likely to demonstrate marked improvements in academic productivity across the early to mid-1990s in Chicago....[S]chools with chronically weak trust reports over this period had virtually no chance of improving in either reading or mathematics."[24]

Bryk and Schneider noted: "We worry that reformers will continue to be frustrated in their efforts unless they meld a stronger organizational view of schools to their otherwise well-conceived initiatives. Good schools are intrinsically social enterprises that depend heavily on cooperative endeavors among the varied participants who comprise the school community. Relational trust constitutes the connective tissue that binds these individuals together around advancing the education and welfare of children. Improving schools requires us to think harder about how best to organize the work of adults and students so that this connective tissue remains healthy and strong." [25]

Further research into relational trust published in 2010 indicated that "when school professionals trust one another and feel supported by parents, they feel safe to experiment with new practices in the classroom and to launch initiatives for reaching out to parents."[26]

Your school

How well does the adult community of your school function? How inclusive is it of cultural differences among staff and in the broader family and extended school community? How is school life for various constituencies, such as specialists, para-professionals, general support staff, administrators, after-school staff, family members, and volunteers? How does adult community morale impact learning and achievement for students?

Current studies in social capital, academic optimism, positive psychology, sociology, multicultural education, and neuroscience add to the evidence that the ways adults work together in schools are likely to deeply influence teacher effectiveness and student learning.[27]

In practice

Elementary Designs learning opportunities for maximizing the collective intelligence and collaborative potential of a school's adult community:

- partnership learning activities (conducive and adaptable for young learners)
- protocols for collaborative conversations for small and large groups
- perspective-taking activities
- establishing and maintaining norms within the adult community
- structures and protocols for meetings
- structures and traditions for engaging families
- democratic school governance

Attuned Student-teacher Relationships

Trusting student-teacher relationships foster attunement and reciprocal learning.

As important as relational trust is in the adult community, it is primary and essential in the classroom. Equity in learning opportunities and achievement thrive on the reciprocal relationship between the teacher and each student. The student must always come first. Juggling a child and a standard, for example, you don't drop the child. In fact, for the child to eventually meet any standard depends on the teacher's presence and belief in the child.

Attunement

The most important data teachers have are those that give insight into each child's family, his or her cultural, developmental, and academic history, and the current situation. Outside the family, you are one of the most important people in the child's life. Attunement with their teachers affords children the emotional safety they need to take risk necessary for growth.[28] Most teachers experience such attunement with at least some of their students, but not all children are able to read the teacher's intent or vice-versa. Stereotypes of culture, language, gender, or other biases may be in the way of deeper connections.

"In order to move forward academically," write researchers Gregory Fouts and John Poulson, "many students seem to need a sense of emotional connection and validation that is brought about by the spontaneous matching and synchronicity of emotions between the teacher and themselves...[but] being in the moment and emotionally communing are impossible to fake; they must be co-created. Some teachers seem to effortlessly promote moments of attunement in the classroom, and these moments flow seamlessly and unite the entire class."[29]

Attunement is not solely intuitive. Teachers can cultivate it through careful observation, communication with family members, other teachers, and with the child. It can also be cultivated through learnable, interactive attunement strategies.[30]

In practice

Elementary Designs practices create reciprocal, culturally aware relationships and attunement with students through:

- beginning-of-school-year goal setting and other conferences with families;
- check-ins with students;
- formative assessment using observation and listening strategies;
- student profiles;
- classroom strategies for establishing traditions and appreciation;
- adult learning experiences in interpersonal mindfulness and attentive collaboration.

Playing to Learn

For children, play is like breathing. Without it, imagination, creativity, spirit, friendliness, curiosity, and interest in learning wither and disappear. Over the past thirty years, we have witnessed the gradual erosion of play in elementary school. Requiring more and more "time on task" increasingly limits children's experiences of self- and other-regulation, spontaneity, taking turns, being surprised, and discovering. Classroom work increasingly focuses on assessments, isolated skill practice (mostly with paper and pencil or electronic tools), direct instruction, and testing, testing, testing, even in preschool.

The good feelings generated when groups of children play and laugh together with their teacher bring loft to learning. Especially for children whose daily experiences may include anxiety, hunger, and fear, play provides refreshment. It is hard to imagine equity in the classroom without fun and play.

This book provides you with numerous ways to maximize the developmental proclivity of young children to play to learn. We hope you will see how important it is to your own love of teaching to play more with your students. As Stuart Brown notes in his definitive work on play, "We are designed to find fulfillment and creative growth through play." [31]

Closing Thoughts: Creating a Polyphonous Classroom

The purpose of this book and the goal of *Elementary Designs* approaches are to support the work of creating educational equity in American elementary schools.

Equity is a crucial and challenging goal for teachers and school leaders. It is an unequivocal necessity for families whose children's education and future are diminished in under-resourced elementary schools.

"Polyphony" is a term used in music to describe two or many voices or sounds coming together to form a nuanced melodic texture, and as applied in literature, to describe the "continuous independence of the voices and viewpoints of the characters" in a text; what author Robert Bringhurst calls "an ecology of voices and a silent voice that arises from the others, speaking on its own of the plurality of being." "The fuel of polyphony is time," writes Bringhurst, "from which it makes the space it needs." [32]

Classrooms and schools can embrace the metaphor of polyphony, taking the time and making the space to allow every voice to be raised, to create a harmonious and rigorous culture of learning, valuing every opinion and perspective, and modeling and respecting the plurality of being—the diverse and authentic democracy we seek for all.

Reading On

In the coming chapters, we examine in detail seven strands of *Elementary Designs* practices for building competence and autonomy, relationship, community structures, and fun. In Chapter Two we focus on building family-school relationships; in Chapter Three on personalized learning; in Chapter Four on whole-class learning that includes and strengthens all learners academically and socially. Chapter Five discusses discipline, scheduling, transitions, and planning. Teaching for equity requires both a broad view and focused work, rigorous yet mindful of children's needs for self-expression, autonomy, and achievement in the context of a supportive community.

Reflection and Next Steps

"The development of the child can reach its highest potential level when education releases and promotes the relevant potential."[33]

Use the space below to jot down thoughts about how to release and promote potential in yourself, in your students, and in your school. As you read on, imagine yourself trying out some of these approaches, or imagine a child you know in a classroom like those we describe. This is a book to be marked up with questions and your own ideas. This is a book leading somewhere. Come along!

1   Bob Katz, *Elaine's Circle: A Teacher, a Classroom, and One Unforgettable Year* (New York: Avon, 2005), 19-20.

2   Today we are repeating a bit of history we must have forgotten. Trying to get children to learn basic skills *earlier* didn't work to close achievement gaps in the 1970's, and it's not likely to work in this go-round with the Common Core Standards. It used to be common pedagogical understanding, for instance, that fourth grade was the year that children made the switch from learning to read to reading to learn. Now teachers are being told that's a third grade transition. Read-alouds of classic children's literature are discouraged in many schools, and teachers are told to put lots of non-fiction and informational texts in the hands of students in grades one through three.

3   See Resources, page 163, for National Center for Education statistics on learning gaps.

4   U.S. Department of Education, "Expansive Survey of America's Public Schools Reveals Troubling Racial Disparities," March 21, 2014. http://www.ed.gov/news/press-releases/expansive-survey-americas-public-schools-reveals-troubling-racial-disparities.

5   Jim Braude, "Broadside: Civil rights challenges of 2014," BroadSide, NCEN.com, January 15, 2014, http://www.necn.com/01/15/14/Broadside-Civil-rights-challenges-of-201/landing_broadside.html?blockID=861809201: Robert Moses in an interview with Jim Braude. See also www.algebra.org.

6   Salman Kahn, *The One World Schoolhouse: Education Reimagined* (Boston: Twelve, 2012), 52.

7   U.S. Department of Education, "Competency-Based Learning or Personalized Learning," ED.gov, http://www.ed.gov/oii-news/competency-based-learning-or-personalized-learning.
    See http://www.bigpicture.org/wp-content/uploads/2011/10/Big-Picture-Brochure.pdf for a wonderful example of this kind of learning at the high school level.

8   Chip Wood, *Time to Teach, Time to Learn: Changing the Pace of School* (Greenfield, MA: Northeast Foundation for Children, 1999).

9   Ruth Charney, Marlynn Clayton, Jay Lord, and Chip Wood, *Notebook for Teachers: Making Changes in the Elementary Curriculum* (Greenfield, MA: Northeast Foundation for Children, 1985, revised edition 1993), 46-49.

10 Galina Zuckerman, "Learning Activity in the First Year of Schooling: The Developmental Path toward Reflection," *Vygotsky's Educational Theory in Cultural Context*, ed. A. Kozulin et al. (New York: Cambridge University Press, 2003), 195-196.

11 Bruce Perry, MD, PhD, "Attunement: Reading the Rhythms of the Child," *Teachers*, Scholastic.com, http://www.scholastic.com/teachers/article/attunement-reading-rhythms-child.

12 See especially Elena Bodrova and Deborah J. Leong, *Tools of the Mind: The Vygotskian Approach to Early Childhood Education*, 2nd ed. (Upper Saddle River, NJ: Pearson, 2007), 40-49.

13 Ibid., 48.

14 Clancy Blair and Cybele Raver, "Closing the Achievement Gap through Modification of Neurocognitive and Neuroendocrine Function: Results from a Cluster Randomized Controlled Trial of an Innovative Approach to Education of Children in Kindergarten." Department of Applied Psychology, Steinhardt School of Culture, Education, and Human Development, New York University (2014 in press), 4.

15 Ibid., 2.

16 Ibid., 13.

17 Galina Zuckerman, "Development of Reflection through Learning Activity," *European Journal of Psychology in Education* vol. xix (2004): 9-18.

18 L.S. Vygotsky, *Mind in Society: Development of Higher Psychological Processes*, ed. Michael Cole, Vera John-Steiner, Sylvia Scribner, and Ellen Souberman (Cambridge, MA: Harvard University Press, 1978), 57.

19 Bodrova and Leong, *Tools of the Mind*, 82.

20 See Acknowledgments, also www.toolsofthemind.org.

21 Parker J. Palmer, *A Hidden Wholeness: Journey toward an Undivided Life* (San Francisco: Jossey-Bass, 2004), 174.

22 Sonia Nieto and Patty Bode, *Affirming Diversity: Sociopolitical Context of Multicultural Education*, 6th ed. (Boston: Pearson, 2012), xv.

23 Bryk and Schneider identified four key aspects of relational trust in school settings: respect, competence, personal regard for others, and integrity. For a definition of each of these, see Resources, page 161-162.

24 Anthony S. Bryk and Barbara Schneider, *Trust in Schools: A Core Resource for Improvement* (New York: B. Russell Sage Foundation, 2004), 123-24.

25 Ibid., 144.

26 Anthony Bryk et al. *Organizing Schools for Improvement: Lessons from Chicago* (Chicago: University of Chicago Press, 2010), 140.

27 See Bibliography: Anrig, Banks, Capps, Darling-Hammond, Dweck, Fredrickson, Goleman, Newberg and Waldman, Nieto, Siegel, Tough, and Wigfield and Eccles.

28 Tina Payne Bryson, "Applying Brain Research to Education: Adult Attachment, Memory and the Whole Brain Child," Responsive Classroom Schools Conference presentation, July 2, 2012. See also Michal Al-Yagon and Mario Mikulincer, *Patterns of Close Relationships and Socioemotional and Academic Adjustment Among School Age Children with Learning Disabilities* (Tel Aviv: Division for Learning Disabilities Research and Practice, 2004): 12-19, http://www.idc.ac.il/publications/files/373.pdf.

29 Gregory Fouts and John Poulsen, "Attunement in the Classroom: Emotional Connections May Be the Key to Student Success," *Alberta Teachers Association Magazine* 81 (2000-01).

30 Luc Stevens, Wim Van Werkoven, and Jos Castelijins, *Attunement Strategy: Reclaiming Children's Motivation by Responsive Instruction* (Geneva: International Bureau of Education, 2001).

31 Stuart Brown, *Play: How it Shapes the Brain, Opens the Imagination, and Invigorates the Soul* (New York: Avery, 2010), 87-88.

32 Robert Bringhurst, "Singing with the Frogs," *Canadian Literature: Contemporary Poetics* no. 155 (Winter 1997): 114-134.

33 Zuckerman, "Learning Activity in the First Year of Schooling," 181.

CHAPTER TWO

Families First

If you ask a parent or caregiver of an elementary school student what they most want for their child and what they most want from the school, you can learn a lot. Here is what a mom of a third grader told me:

"I want my daughter to be educated to read and write and be competent in the world, but more than that I want her to be in a place where she is taught, nourished and honored. What I mean by that is that I want her to have the basic skills, but what I really want is for her to spend time where she is equally nourished as at home but in areas that home doesn't specialize in.

"It's also the school's responsibility to bring in education that would meet any diversity that might walk into the school. My child is a child of color, but this should be provided not just for her but for all children. Teaching about the cultures of the world is not only good for the children who carry those diverse traits.

"I want her to come out competent, empowered with her own knowledge, to be able to hold a conversation, and talk about what she believes to be true."

A dad of a child not yet school age told me: "I went to all African-American schools with African-American teachers and staff. I did fine in elementary school. My mom helped out at school and helped me at home when I was young. But that all changed in middle school. I was put in a resource room because of behavior, and then I was kept back in the seventh grade. I didn't know why. I dropped out at thirteen and later started to pursue adult education online and through a school run by the National Guard and later got my high school diploma online. I realized I needed to learn on my own.

"Thinking about my daughter, I want her to be able to learn a real academic experience, learning to use numbers and letters as opposed just going to school to just be entertained for eight hours a day. I expect the school system to do a good job, but also I would have her further her learning at home. Diverse education is important to me. I do worry about my child learning biased history. I would like her to know the whole story of history.

"I don't want my daughter to be upset that she is of color or has curly hair. I don't want her to have to deal with this in schools, and I know I can't protect her... I expect the school to take care of her like I would, keep her from being bullied. All the teachers and staff, I would expect them to do that."

Families call for autonomy, competence, relationship, community, and play

The elementary requirements that we introduced in Chapter One speak to the expectations and hopes the two parents expressed in the quotes above. Parents and caretakers often use phrases like "strong and independent," "knowing how to read and write about stuff that matters," "know her ABC's," "know how to get along," "have fun and come home with a smile on her face about something she learned," "be a friend," "learn how to take care of himself," "get to move around, not just sit still all day," and "like school" to express their commitment to what we call the basic needs of children: autonomy, competence, relationship, community, and play. These basic needs must be considered and addressed in order for all children to learn successfully.

School-family engagement becomes meaningful when adults in the school and caregivers at home have many opportunities to communicate their understandings about each other's goals and aspirations for the children and for their success in school, with appreciation and respect for different points of view. This requires time for making personal connections, clear communication, and school practices that support such engagement.

In this chapter, we

- offer strategies for family engagement that can be integrated into the curriculum and flow of the classroom day, as well as into the organizational structure and traditions of your school
- offer models from schools, including those where we've held leadership roles, to consider how others have brought concerns for equity and commitment to their particular communities and situations.

A Principal's Story

I walked the halls late one spring with a staff member of an elementary school where I soon would be taking over as principal. I had just been hired, and it had been years since my previous principalship—years spent in many schools, coaching and consulting and leading workshops and family forums. Over some twenty years, I had learned a lot by being in so many different schools, but I also knew I had a lot to figure out about the school into which I was stepping. There had been quite a large hiring committee, but I felt that families were under-represented both in number and in representation of various cultural segments of the community, half of whose families were living below the poverty line.

The school had experienced a rapid turnover in principals during the previous decade. The hiring committee had told me their first priority was school climate and culture. Family participation was low and student behavior was troubling. Teachers were dedicated, but they were weary of one- or two-year leaders and wary of new initiatives.

I asked the teacher I was walking with, "When do families find out what class their children are in next year? Do they already know?" The teacher explained that teachers made step-up recommendations about children they had taught in the current year to the next grade-level teachers, who met with them and then divided the students into classes to create an academic and behavioral balance and mix of students in each classroom. The principal had a final look, and class lists were posted on the doors of the school at some point during the summer. I filed that information away as we continued our tour of the building. During my five-year tenure as principal of the school, we didn't do all we could have to fully engage families in the school, but we worked at it steadily as a community and through procedural changes. We developed useful approaches to turning a school toward being the learning village it needs to be. I'll come back to these approaches later in the chapter.

Doubtless, you have many local traditions, special events, and daily practices that help involve families in the life of your school. As you read this chapter, take time to consider what might broaden participation at your school and to think about the part you might play in making this happen.

Starting Points

How might you best approach your ongoing work with your school families? According to the authors of *Beyond the Bake Sale: The Essential Guide to Family-School Partnerships*, the answer depends on where your school is currently in partnering with families.[1]

We've included a useful rubric from *Beyond the Bake Sale* (see page 166 in Resources) to help you consider your school's efforts. The rubric is clear, focusing on five areas: Building Relationships; Linking to Learning; Addressing Differences; Supporting Advocacy; and Sharing Power. Your assessment of your school from your perspective, as well as from those of families and school staff, will likely tell you a lot. I wish I had come across this book before we started working on increasing family-school engagement at my school!

Teaching for equity in our classrooms and schools requires communicating our commitment to each family of the students we teach. We do not know whether there is a moment of realization for each family that a school really cares about them and their children's needs. Furthermore, mutual engagement between school and home cannot guarantee positive results in academic and social growth for every single child. But we know from studies and our own experience that the more frequently positive and meaningful exchanges occur between school personnel and family members, the better for young learners.[2] It's logical to extend the personalized learning that we facilitate in the classroom to significant, personalized communication with families.

First, let's look at what teachers can do in their relationships with families, followed by a broader examination of opportunities for other school personnel.

Approaches to Personalized Family Communication with Teachers

Here are six interrelated approaches for teachers and administrators to consider:

1. Goal-setting conferences between families and teachers before school begins
2. Recognition of student growth
3. Student-teacher check-ins
4. Yes! cards to families
5. Additional family-focused conferences during the school year
6. Keeping report cards in perspective.

Goal-setting conferences between families and teachers before school begins

These conferences before school begins can set a high standard for partnership. If it is not possible to have them before the first day of school, then the purpose of these conferences can be introduced and explained at class meetings during Open House in September or as early as possible in the school year. Goal-setting sheets can be picked up in the child's classroom at Open House, or they can be mailed home. Goal setting is part of the first formal family-teacher conference, usually held in late fall. Approaches to recording and sharing growth with families, including the use of Yes! cards, are explained during this first conference. *Elementary Designs* practice suggests two or three family-teacher conferences during the school year, whether or not conferences before school begins are part of your family-school engagement plan.

The Regional Multicultural Magnet School (RMMS) is a 523-student K-5 school that draws diverse learners from 17 surrounding towns into New London, Connecticut. The school calendar includes two days before classes begin in late summer for each teacher to meet with the students of his or her incoming class and their families. The objective of these half-hour conferences is "to focus on the child as a person and a learner and the important connection between school and home. The child, with input from the teacher and parent/caregiver, develops one or two goals for the school year. These goals are continually revisited throughout the school year." Earlier in the summer, families receive information packets for the new school year, including a copy of a School-Family Compact and suggestions from the teacher to help with setting goals with and for the children.[3]

Example family conference

At a March follow-up family conference, third grader Emily, her mother, and her teacher discuss her progress toward goals set together back in August. Emily has been in teacher Sue Goldstein's bilingual classroom since second grade. This is one of RMMS's two-year looping bilingual tracks. Emily is friendly, engaging, and positive in the conference. She is delighted that her mother and her teacher are happy with what she has to share. The following is transcribed from video footage of the conference.

Ms. Goldstein begins by bringing out Emily's original goal sheet and reviews her goals and "action steps" with her.

1. Learning math facts—practice my facts
2. More confidence in math—help K-1 students in math
3. Complete work on time—develop confidence and responsibility check.

Emily, her mom, and the teacher agree that regular practice with flash cards is still needed. Ms. Goldstein asks Emily's mother, "Do you see her confidence increasing?" "Yes, I do!" she replies. Ms. Goldstein shows Emily her social-emotional goal: "To continue your happy, healthy spirit." Emily grins. "Do you see that at home, too?" asks Ms. Goldstein. Mom and daughter smile at each other.

"What do you think about doing the math facts on the iPad or flash cards?" inquires the mother. There is a little discussion about this and then she comments, "She likes to read. She's borrowing books from her friends in the classroom and I like that."

Ms. Goldstein takes this cue to have Emily read some poetry to her mom and quizzes Emily to see if she knows what the word "spade" means, prompting her to use context clues from the pictures. She then has her read a few pages in Spanish, noting to her mom that Emily is more fluent in English and suggests maybe she could read more in Spanish to her mother. "Practice with her," she says, smiling.

Emily then shares about her "word memoir" that she is going to read to the whole school (all of her classmates will share their memoirs). She is proud of it: "It's something that quickly tells other people how I feel about something. Mine is, 'Reading is like food to me.'"

Toward the end of the conference time, Ms. Goldstein talks a little about the new computer testing third graders are taking for the first time and asks Emily, "What can you do if you feel stressed at testing time?" Emily answers, "You can center or you can stretch," two things they learned this year.

"Fourth grade next year, can you believe it?!" Ms. Goldstein asks Emily's mother. "I can't! I just can't!" she replies. To her daughter she says, "I'm very proud of you."

Recognition of student growth

A progress account is a running list of a child's accomplishments, a ledger in which students and their families see the evidence of growth in personal learning and ways that children have demonstrated either incremental success or proficiency by, for instance, a high score on a test, or demonstrating the ability to do long division. The accomplishment doesn't prove that the child has completely mastered the skill, but that he has shown proficiency in it. He can keep revisiting the core ideas and skills through different, active experiences such as teaching the skill to another student. That's the way to get the holes out of what Salman Kahn calls "Swiss cheese learning."[4]

What does this have to do with family engagement? By seeing on a regular basis that their child is making progress in skill development and is, in the language of personalized learning, moving on to new challenges, parents and caregivers have continuous evidence of both their child's growth and the pace of that growth. This is an important shift in understanding for students, teachers, and families. Rather than being moved along with the class, ready or not, families are assured that their children are working toward proficiency as they travel the spiral staircase of modern curricula. At conferences and through other communications, they can see that their child's teacher is committed to his or her growth and will provide multiple opportunities for the child to practice with teachers, tutors, and teaching assistants, retake tests and quizzes, and target homework toward developing skills.

Student-teacher check-ins

Teachers have many things to take under consideration as they help children to reflect on and revise their goals over the school year. At RMMS in the example above, these include grade and developmental levels, language development (RMMS offers a section of Spanish-immersion classrooms), special needs, learning differences, and emerging special strengths.

In *Elementary Designs* practices, we encourage teachers to check in frequently with students so the teacher can monitor progress toward some immediate goal on any given day. Check-ins, which last just two to five minutes, are facilitated by 1) student folders that reflect progress toward goals and/or incremental success toward mastery of a specific skill, all part of students' growth records, and 2) Yes! cards sent home to families.

Yes! cards to families

Checking progress in achievement ledgers and student folders, you can prepare a Yes! card to send home, ready for posting on the refrigerator door. See a full discussion of these cards in Chapter Three. Yes! cards can regularly inform family members of their child's academic and social growth. Consider using the categories below and commenting on:

Connecting (Relationship)

- Effective connecting with peer partners, teachers, support staff
- Someone they helped, tutored, or stood up for
- Someone they worked with and what they learned
- Someone who taught them something

Understanding (Competence)

- Skills they have mastered
- Something they taught someone else
- A new goal
- Something they made, invented, and/or presented

Deciding (Autonomy)

- A decision they made and what they learned from making it
- Something for which they took personal responsibility
- Something they did on their own and were proud of
- Something they learned because they were curious or made a mistake
- A time when they assumed leadership and did well

Any time teacher or family concerns arise, direct contact is made as soon as possible and a time to meet in person or talk on the phone is arranged.

Family-focused conferences during the school year

Traditional family-teacher conferences have three common weaknesses: they are too brief, teachers do most of the talking, and goal setting is rarely involved. By holding the first family-focused conference before school begins, all three of these issues are addressed: the conference is planned for half an hour; the teacher starts the conference by asking the family to talk about themselves; and family members and the child come to the conference with goals in mind. This creates a structure for three formal meetings during the school year.

Below are some ideas for structuring conferences. Each school and grade level will construct their own design and schedule based on local conditions such as time allotted for conferences contractually, district requirements around interpreting report cards and sharing test results, and other mandates.

For each conference, we recommend that: [5]

1. Students attend conferences with their families

While there may sometimes be a need for parents or caregivers to meet privately with a teacher, specialist, or administrator, in most conferences having the student present shows transparency and shared accountability and pride for all involved. Teachers engage students in rehearsal prior to conferences so they can practice their role in sharing information with families. The rehearsal changes to match the different student roles in conferences over the year. There are ways to facilitate a few minutes of the conference just for adults if necessary, by arranging a room or rooms for the students to go to, staffed by adults, for refreshments, books, and/or crafts, where the adults will join them a little later. Otherwise, the teacher and caregivers may schedule another time to meet, especially if it is important for specialists or administrators to be present.

2. The conference opens with an invitation for family members to speak first

This simple flip of the usual protocol has made remarkable differences in family-teacher relationships where it has been tried. Families have recounted their positive feelings about being listened to, not just talked to, by the teacher.

3. Teacher emphasizes positive growth

It is difficult to avoid reporting on the skills the child is struggling with, but the conference needs to focus on the positive, because when parents and teachers both focus on what students are learning and their persistence in their school work, further positive achievement and growth will result. [6]

4. The teacher utilizes goal setting to address concerns and perceived deficits

Goal setting with students and family members (described above, re: the before-school conference) is a strategy for agreement by all involved on high standards and the capacity of the student to master skills through personalized learning and realistic, incremental success (see Chapter Three: Personalized Learning).

5. At the end of the conference, the teacher summarizes what was said, next steps, and appreciations
Reflection is a strategy and a skill that helps solidify learning in memory. It also provides formal closure.

Late fall family conference

- This serves as the goal-setting conference, if it has not already occurred
- The family is asked to bring stories of three school-related things they have talked about at home:
  1) Something the child has accomplished and is proud of
  2) People, including classmates, the child has learned from
  3) Anything the child or family is concerned about
- The conference's first ten minutes focus on what the family brings and is led by the family
- The conference's second ten minutes are led by the teacher to share the report card and/or the student's growth record
- The last ten minutes of the conference are for dialogue, goal setting, appreciations, and summarizing

Winter family conference

- The family is asked to bring
  1) Something to share about their family traditions and culture
  2) Anything the child or family is worried about
- The conference's first ten minutes focus on what the family has brought and is led by the family
- The conference's second ten minutes are led by the teacher, with the child sharing from his/her growth records
- The last ten minutes are for mutual goal setting, appreciations, and summarizing

Spring family conference

- The family is asked to bring
  1) Additions for a classroom poster display or list of families' highlights during the school year (to be added to a poster in the classroom)
  2) Anything the child or family is worried about
- The conference's first ten minutes focus on what the family has brought and can be led by the student
- The conference's second ten minutes are led by the student, sharing from his/her growth records and work samples with support from the teacher
- The last ten minutes are led by the teacher to share her assessment and summary of the student's growth over the year and possibly to share the report card.

Keeping report cards in perspective

Many school districts seem to be in a state of constant revision of their report card process.

Behind every wave of new standards and new curriculum come new and more complex report cards to explain student achievement along a continuum of learning according to grade-level benchmarks. These are not always easy for parents and caregivers to understand. The computerized reports they receive usually sort student progress by subject into categories such as *Warning, Needs Improvement, Proficient,* and *Advanced,* mirroring the reporting language of high-stakes tests. Specific basic skills are listed in each subject area using similar terminology.

Computer programs generate report cards based on data entered by teachers into computer grade books which in turn go into a district computer. The district program provides teachers with an extensive menu of comments that might describe student performance, effort, and difficulties, as well as room for a teacher's sentence or two to personalize the report. Although limited, the latter opportunity to personalize can be meaningful.

What report cards don't do

Most report cards provide information about where the child stands in comparison to other students at the same grade level in the same school; in the district; and in the state. In reality, at the end of a marking period (or at any other moment), students are at various points on the continuum of learning, and most will have *different rates of growth* on that continuum that are rarely reflected on report cards. For instance, a student who is graded as *Needs Improvement* in reading in the fall or winter marking period may have mastered many critical concepts and skills by the spring, and is making rapid progress toward grade level proficiency. However, the grade given to the student may be interpreted as a "D" or a failing grade by parents or caregivers, and they may think their student isn't working hard, or, worse, isn't capable of learning.

Report cards and equity

Educators teaching for equity and using *Elementary Designs* strategies need to make sure at report card times to share with families the student's growth record and to give them a complete assessment of outcomes for the student by the end of the school year. Above all, the teacher reinforces and helps the parents or caregivers reinforce with the child every positive growth indicator. This is key to sustaining a growth mindset for student, family, and teacher and realizing the best possible outcomes by the end of the year.

Whole-school Approaches to Family Engagement

So far we have considered classroom-centered strategies, where teachers carry the responsibility. Often responsibility for communication and partnership with the families starts and stops with classroom interactions. But supporting and sustaining strong family engagement and partnership is part of many people's responsibilities (it takes a village!), extending beyond student-teacher interactions.

Each classroom teacher communicates with 25, 30, or more families throughout the school year, which may include multiple parents, guardians, or caregivers in separated, divorced, blended, and extended families. S/he sends home a welcome letter, weekly folders with notices about school events, homework assignments, lunch-money forms, children's completed work, and so on. Families have access to the teacher's school e-mail and, in most cases, to a Web page for the class. S/he hosts at least two brief conferences to discuss report cards and other progress reports and observations, s/he meets with family members who request a conference at any time to discuss any concern, and s/he attends special-education meetings for children receiving special services. Her classroom cohort of students and families will change as families come and go during the year.

And this is not all s/he is responsible for! Most of a teacher's time is spent teaching, creating lesson plans, assigning, correcting, and reviewing student work, testing, assessing student strengths and weaknesses, arranging extra support for struggling students, planning and leading field trips (when budgets allow), attending school and family events, and attending professional-development events, grade-level meetings, committee meetings, and whole-faculty meetings (we no doubt left a few things out!).

Family engagement roles beyond classroom teachers

How does a school really put families first? How can everyone take on the commitment and fulfill their role? How are roles coordinated? Let's look at some of the roles other school staff have in connecting with and supporting families.

The *school secretary*, "the face of the school," is often the first person families encounter. S/he must listen carefully and know whom to connect the family with first.

Families may communicate with the *school nurse* first thing in the morning. Depending on the size of the school, the nurse will see dozens or scores of children for health-related issues each day, needing to communicate with parents, guardians, and caregivers as well as with teachers, secretaries, social workers, and the principal.

The *social worker or school counselor* coordinates services with public agencies, prepares and presents classroom lessons on anti-bullying, personal safety, making good decisions, and so on. S/he leads individual and group therapeutic sessions and communicates with teachers about children's issues, and talks with parents, guardians, and caregivers. Specific concerns about student learning or behavior may be referred to a student support team meeting which s/he may attend.

The *principal*, an authority figure, is the person parents, guardians, and caregivers speak with about discipline, concerns about teachers or staff, and school policy.

The *extended day program director*, on or off site, may be the person with the closest connections to school families. S/he may be a volunteer, a youth worker, or a community agency employee. S/he is likely to know all the children from a particular family attending the school, including extended family.

Special-education teachers, physical therapists, social workers, paraprofessionals, behavioral interventionists, and other personnel all have reason to be in communication with families of the children they serve directly.

The coordination of work with families is usually the responsibility of the principal, and it may be a part of regular leadership meetings where grade-level representatives and specialists share information about family concerns, meetings, events, conferences, community resources, or school issues.

If the school is lucky enough to have a family volunteer coordinator, that person may serve as the point person for events, volunteer placements, and feedback from families. Sometimes the head of the Family-Teacher Organization or of the school council may be invited to a leadership team meeting. Other means of coordination of these roles is presented in three school models later in the chapter.

Poverty and family engagement

In the elementary school where I was most recently the principal, many on our staff lacked a key awareness for deepening family engagement: a realistic and thorough understanding of the grinding, daily impact of poverty on our students and families. We also needed greater awareness of what families could teach us from their cultural perspectives about teaching their children. As in many schools, there was a disconnect between the lived experiences of school professionals and school families. Every teacher and administrator in the school was middle class, while nearly 60% of the families of students were eligible for free or reduced-price lunch. Nearly 90% of the eligible families were white and poor. A small number of them were recent, white immigrants or Latino migrant workers. Some of our support staff and teachers who grew up in the area had a closer connection to community needs than some specialists, service providers, and administrators, but their perspectives were not always heard. Personal opinions and value judgments about such things as child rearing sometimes displaced communication and problem-solving. Working with families was nobody's top priority, nor were any staff members trained or specifically assigned to work with families.

Facing the odds

I was responsible for moving the school toward more family engagement, and I knew that certain conversations were essential for us: namely, tough discussions about equity.

There are so many important things to do! I was often involved in emergency triage, seeking resources, making referrals, talking to social-service agencies, and responding to families' immediate needs; where was the time for the relationship building necessary for a true school-family partnership? In a so-called "underperforming" school like ours, educators can get overwhelmed by the initiatives and mandates of the day, by testing and scores, and by external monitoring.

We saw and discussed the challenges children were facing, and we saw the odds we faced in striving for equity in educational outcomes without adequate resources. It was very difficult to reach and teach many students with so much acting-out behavior, anger, frustration, and fear present in classrooms. We put good programs in place, including before and after school. Nevertheless, the school was put on a state list for student underperformance and not meeting AYP one year, and the next year was recognized as a State Commendation School for its significant statistical progress toward AYP.

No good work unpunished

Ironically, our achievement caused a decrease in the amount of state aid for students the next year, and the year after that, test results fell back. We continued to put "oxygen masks" (extra attention) on the neediest students before attending to the "crew" (the adult community), and the crew, stretched thin, paid less attention to the needs of the rest of the "passengers" (the students).

Clearly, more time and staff were needed for us to respond to and empower families to deal with the consequences of poverty. We especially needed training and skills to adequately engage with families in difficult, sometimes traumatic circumstances induced by poverty, but they were not forthcoming. Despite the staff's care and concern for the students, and despite an active and positively recognized school-community council that included key social agencies in this low-income community, the school did not receive enough support for educators and staff to deepen their cultural competence and learn positive strategies to respond to all students and families in the community.

Cultural gaps

Teachers and administrators are increasingly distanced and disassociated from those at the margins by the widening discrepancies between students and teachers in gender, "race," and economic class:

- "[B}y 2020, the percentage of teachers of color will fall to five percent, while the percentage of students of color in the system will likely exceed 50 percent."[7]
- The percentage of female K-12 teachers increased to an all-time high in 2011 of 84%, with males dropping to just 16%.[8]
- The number of children in poverty in this country, the vast majority of whom attend public schools, reached 16 million in 2012.
  - 40%, or 6.4 million, of these children lived in extreme poverty, defined for a family of four as income of $11,746 or less.

- One in five children were living in poverty in 2012, two-thirds of whom lived in families with at least one working family member.
- 5.8 million children in poverty were Latino American, 5.2 million were European American, and 4.1 million were African American.
- One-third of children living in poverty were children of color. The average income of all households in the United States in 2011 was $81,199 for Asian Americans, $75,448 for European Americans, $36, 949 for Latino Americans, and $35,665 for African Americans.
- The poverty line for a family of four in 2012 was $23,492.[9]

Cultural gaps between teachers and families in public elementary schools also generate increasingly divergent and sometimes more segregated life experiences. Writing on empathy and cultural competence, educator and writer Michaela Columbo notes, "As students themselves, most teachers were socialized in mainstream schools for at least 12 years and often attended teacher-preparation programs grounded in the mainstream culture. In (child care) centers and schools, many teachers then find themselves working with colleagues who have similar educational and professional experiences.

"Beginning the journey toward increased cultural competence (the ability to understand diverse perspectives and appropriately interact with members of other cultures in a variety of situations) requires teachers to rethink their assumptions and consider life's issues through the lenses of people who come from cultural backgrounds different from their own."[10] The overwhelming majority of elementary educators today are white and female. We hope that as the percentage of students of color moves from 50% upward, the percentage of teachers and administrators of color in elementary education will increase significantly, bringing additional cultural perspectives to the teaching profession.

In the personalized approaches of *Elementary Designs*, teachers and administrators are led to reflect, consider, and explore classroom and school practices to enhance their cultural understanding.

Community-specific aspect of family-school engagement

Building a truly representative, inclusive, and democratic decision-making management structure for an elementary school is a challenge, as is maintaining an effective communication network for families and school personnel. The structures that exist in your school today are nested in the legal authority of the school district, its policies and procedures, and layers of decision-making and bureaucracy. It takes patience, perseverance, and savvy to develop and nurture meaningful multicultural understanding and relationships among all the constituencies in a school community, but it is well worth the trouble. Such relationships encourage students and families to trust and participate in the school's commitment to equity in learning outcomes.

Much depends on the culture of your school and the cultures in your community. Following are some family-engagement approaches to consider. First, we return to my story from page 37 when I was principal.

Family Engagement Approaches from My Principal Experience

Welcome

Every time we increased the "welcome quotient" (WQ) in our school, we increased trust. Through summer family events, picnics, parades, ceremonies, meet-and-greets, orientations, and community coffee klatches we reached out to as many families as we could. Our non-teaching staff were indispensable in these efforts. Their spirit, energy, friendliness, and helpfulness set a tone of eager participation throughout the building. Our school secretaries got to know families and welcomed them whenever they showed up. The smiles, greetings, and how-can-I-help-you's of our custodians, cafeteria workers, para-professionals, crossing guards, and before- and after-school staff made a big difference to families.

Empowerment

Parents and caregivers who have a request or question about their child's class placement deserve to be heard and responded to in a timely manner. When language was a barrier to communication in our school, our ELL teacher and our home liaison assisted, and they made sure families understood the school's procedures. While class placement couldn't always be guaranteed because of the many factors that determine class makeup, we seriously considered each request. It took more time and didn't always work out for every family, but our *invitation* to communicate showed respect and caring about what families wanted for their children.[11] For similar reasons, families appreciated receiving class-placement letters in spring or early summer.

Engagement

Mutual understanding about student discipline is critical to a healthy school culture and family trust. Our school invited families to engage with us in conversations about discipline, because there were differences between home and school practices, as there are in most school communities. Having parents and caregivers join with us in discussing and reaching agreement on school-wide discipline protocols helped create common language, mutual understanding, and an increased sense of fairness in all sectors of the school community.[12]

Friendliness

Our school handbook was family-friendly, dotted with student artwork and photos that highlighted the diversity of the community. We provided clear, succinct explanations of school procedures and requirements and a description of our positive approach to school discipline, as well as the practices we utilized as consequences for student misbehavior, and how behavior incidents would be communicated to families.

Agency

We invited and recruited families to help develop and strengthen our Title I school compact through our school council. This broadened democratic participation of family members. At the open house in September, we got ideas and volunteers from families, and we had PTO officers help family members fill out nomination papers for school council elections. All of these practices increased participation from a broader spectrum of the family community in our school. School Council and family-teacher organization meetings became settings for practicing participatory democracy, and they were opportunities to share ideas and opinions and to take action on important school matters. Meanwhile, teachers and administrators made sure to keep in touch with these school organizations through regular personal contact.

Invitation

Maximizing the possibilities for family participation during before- and after-school programming expands the sense of welcome and inclusion in school. For instance, we sought and received funds from a service organization to provide transportation for a before-school grandparents' breakfast. We expected after-school staff to invite family members in for a quick tour of a learning activity at pick-up time at the end of the day. And our school counselor created Career Day, which highlighted community jobs and relatives who worked in them.

Family Engagement Approaches at RMMS

At the Regional Multicultural Magnet School, 47% of the students qualify for free lunch or a reduced lunch rate. 10% of the students have special needs; 16% are ELL students; 41% are European American, 32% Latin American, 16% two or more "race" categories, 8% African American, and 5% Asian American. Reporting to the regional administration and school board, the school created this common vision and set of practices for family engagement:

"As a school community and culture, partnership with families is embedded in all that we do. We truly believe that each child belongs to all of us and it takes a whole village to raise each child. Every staff member at the Regional Multicultural Magnet School is an advocate for your child.

"RMMS is committed to:
- Open lines of communication with families
- Contact with parents/caregivers on a regular basis
- Contact with parents/caregivers as soon as there is a problem
- Involving parents/caregivers in their child's school work and life
- Involving parents/caregivers in the life of the school
- Finding support for families in crisis
- Helping network parents/caregivers for transportation to school events
- Bringing parental concerns forward within the school community to determine if there is a broader school issue."

This vision is backed up by a network of school personnel who support family-school engagement, and the school enjoys enthusiastic family participation at all levels:
- **COMPASS (COMMUNITY, PLANNING, ACCOUNTABILITY, SPIRIT AND STEERING):** A family-staff organization
- **RMMS STEERING COMMITTEE:** Family representatives, staff representatives by grade level, and support staff constituencies; COMPASS members are welcome.
- **BEHAVIORAL AND EMOTIONAL SUPPORT TEAM (BEST):** This team is comprised of a behavioral support specialist, a behavioral support instructor, a school social worker, a community-based social worker, the school nurse, the school associate director, and the school director. This team also supports the work of the Child Study Team and its process of formal assessment and review of students needing support, conducted with families, teachers, and support staff. [13]

In this example of family engagement, an intentional interlocking network of committees invites a degree of overlapping membership, with a certain amount of redundancy of purpose. Some families may find one setting a good fit for their interests, while another finds a resource for meeting their child's needs, and another a place where they can bring a new idea to propose to the school. Attracting a significant percentage of families from the diversity of the school community into participation requires personal invitation, recruitment, and welcome to each segment of the community. Families should be invited to all types of meetings of the school community (not just the FTO and student presentations, for example), with translation services, convenient meeting times, childcare, transportation, and attractions, such as food and a student presentation or academic sharing to start every meeting, no matter what the topic.

If the classroom is the cradle of democracy, parents and caregivers, teachers, staff, and other community members have the hearts and hands that must lovingly rock the cradle to demonstrate the promise of democracy and of equity for all children. In a study of school change in Chicago, a part of which looked at what contributed to a seven-year trend of improved reading scores in some previously low-achieving schools, it was found that one of the most distinctive features in these schools was a more effective local school council.[14]

Family Engagement Approaches at Union City

Union City, New Jersey, fosters strong family-school-community partnerships, as chronicled in David L. Kirp's 2013 book, *Improbable Scholars: The Rebirth of a Great American School System and a Strategy for America's Schools.*

Key features of the Union City approach:

- "The culture of *abrazos*, love and caring, at Washington School is rooted in close relationships of long standing between Les [the principal] and the teachers, and between the school and the families. These professionals know and trust one another, for they can draw on their history of working together, and that eases the path to collaboration. Their ties to the kids come naturally because they have an intimate understanding of their students' lives."

- A significant percentage of teachers, staff, and administrators are of similar ethnic and cultural backgrounds as the students

- Teachers and administrators have stayed at their schools for a long time together
- "High-quality, full-day preschool starting for all children at three.
- Immigrant students become fluent first in their native language and then in English.
- Teachers and students get hands-on help to improve their performance.
- The schools reach out to families, enlisting them as partners in their children's education." [15]

Many family-school partnerships mean well, but in Union City, vigilance, looking after the well-being of each student, is a responsibility shared between families and schools.

Family Advocates: A Way Forward

Putting families first in schools requires nimble thinking and action and creative budgeting and time management. Key to success is finding ways to create efficiency and accountability across the shared responsibilities.

In Iowa City, Iowa, elementary schools employ full-time student and family advocates who report to their building principal and to the coordinator of mental health services in the district. "The role of the Student and Family Advocate is to support students in achieving the following outcomes: (1) enhanced pro-social behaviors, (2) increased school attendance, and (3) positive school connectedness. The Student and Family Advocate is utilized to provide individual student support, promote parent engagement and act as a liaison between school, parents and community resources in order to enhance student learning, promote the overall efficiency of the school system, and maximize the educational opportunities available to each child."[16] (Advocates are professional positions within the district with an extensive job description, *solely focused on student and family support.*)

Iowa City began their student and family advocate program 18 years ago and now receives funds from three municipalities and a federal Safe Schools, Healthy Schools grant, according to coordinator Joan Vandenberg, who says, "We have learned how enormously important it is to have an access point for families, and the student and family advocates are just that. They are the hub." Vandenberg also told me that as a result of having advocates, families see that the schools will help them and that they can get lots of resources by talking with advocates. She said most advocates have social-work backgrounds and provide a strong communication link for teachers as well as for families.

The Shoreline School District in the State of Washington describes a family advocacy department serving nine elementary schools and two centers. A brochure explains:

"The Family Advocate at your school can provide support to you in many different ways. Every child and family is unique and will have different strengths and needs. Here are some ways the Family Advocate might be of assistance to you:

- Provide general information and clarification about the school
- Collaborate with you and school staff to improve your child's learning and school performance
- Connect your family to resources in the school community
- Advocate for you or your child to receive needed services
- Provide social, emotional, and behavioral support for your child at school
- Provide support and resources to your child and family in times of crisis"[17]

We advocate and cheerlead for school family advocates to become commonplace in the field of education. The school districts we have talked to who have taken this bold, wise, and pioneering step are demonstrating a deep understanding and acknowledgment of what it takes to stand behind a commitment to the real possibility of equity of outcomes for every student in their districts.[18]

How many years might it take in education for family advocates to sit on school leadership teams and to represent their school and individual families wherever necessary in the broader community? This is the leading edge of school-family partnership, a pathway to equity. Perhaps as family advocates become more prevalent in schools, a new professional path analogous to that of Family Nurse Practitioners in the field of medicine may emerge in education.[19]

What the advocate does

An important benefit of having a school family advocate is coordination of information and referral services within the school and with families. An elementary school of 500 students may actually be a school of, say, 325 or fewer families. The advocate can consolidate support for all 500 students by working with the 325 families. If a family is in need of multiple services or is in crisis, many people need to be informed. Perhaps the advocate could be on the school leadership team for the school to gain the greatest benefit.

A family advocate can serve as the hub for referrals and information needed by special services, counselors and social workers, classroom teachers and administrators. S/he does not provide direct services, but advocates for families and helps them get the services they need. S/he can also expedite the family's getting direct services by providing initial information and referral to service providers.

Rearranging these functions requires a cultural shift in schools, but the benefits of having these workers in schools might be as transformative for family-school engagement as it is for family preventive health care.

Extended assistance for families

Rebecca Onie, who as a college student volunteered in a clinic, saw the connection between poverty and poor health: many people who lived in poverty were sick as a result of being poor. They lacked sufficient heat in the winter; they couldn't afford healthful food and made do with empty calories; families were chronically anxious about gathering money for the next month's rent. Doctors prescribed medicine and lines of treatment but these prescriptions did not address the underlying health-threatening issues of hunger and other basic survival needs. When she finished college, Onie went on to create Health Leads, a nonprofit that fills prescriptions from healthcare providers for basic necessities like food and heat. Healthcare professionals refer patients to Health Leads just as they do any other specialty. Now operating in six American cities, Health Leads recruits and trains college students to fill these prescriptions by connecting patients with the basic resources they need to be healthy.[20]

Imagine if every elementary school had a "health desk" in a room next to the nurse's office or in a private space in the school office staffed by college volunteers, perhaps trained by Health Leads and overseen by the school family advocate, or a team like the BEST Team at RMMS. Family engagement would be even more effective in creating the conditions and fulfilling the elementary requirements for equal opportunities to learn.

Reflection and Next Steps

No school can implement all of the ideas offered in this chapter about family engagement all at once. The idea that grabbed your attention may not be the one that excited the teacher next door or the administrator down the hall, or the head of the FTO, but it may be just right for you to think more about, try out on your own, or recommend to your principal or professional learning community or grade-level team. Later, perhaps you will bring it up for consideration at the school level.

Here are some questions for your reflection:

What in this chapter got you thinking about your part in family engagement? What is something you may want to try?

What is something you read that you may want to bring to the attention of someone in your school?

While reading the chapter, what family or families did it bring to mind that you might want to connect with?

Who from your school community might you want to acknowledge for their work with families, or what family you would like to thank for what they do for the school?

Look back on how you assessed your school in the self-scoring rubric from *Beyond the Bake Sale* (introduced on page 38, rubric on pages 166-170)What next steps do you think the school should take? Whom might you mention this to?

1   Anne T. Henderson, Karen L. Mapp, Vivian R. Johnson, and Don Davies, *Beyond the Bake Sale: Essential Guide to Family-School Partnerships* (New York: New Press, 2007), 13-25. See Resources, pages 166-170, for the self-scoring rubric.
2   Jung-Sook Lee and Natasha K. Bowen, "Parent Involvement, Cultural Capital, and the Achievement Gap Among Elementary School Children" *American Educational Research Journal* 43, no. 2 (Summer 2006): 193-218.
3   Personal correspondence, Paul Carolan, RMMS Director, February, 2014.

4   Salman Kahn, *The One World Schoolhouse: Education Reimagined* (Boston: Twelve, 2012), 84.
5   Read about the benefits of more student- and family-involved conference structures at http://blogs.edweek.org/edweek/finding_common_ground/2011/11/student-led_conferences.html.
6   Natasha Cabrera, "Positive Development of Minority Children: Social Policy Report," *Sharing Child and Youth Development Knowledge* 27 no. 2 (2013).
7   The Woodrow Wilson National Fellowship Foundation, "Tomorrow's Students Urgently Need Teachers of Color," http://woodrow.org/fellowships/ww-rbf-fellowships/.
8   C. Emily Feistritzer, "Profile of Teachers in the U.S. 2011," National Center for Education Information, http://www.edweek.org/media/pot2011final-blog.pdf.
9   Children's Defense Fund, "The State of America's Children 2014," 22-23, http://www.childrensdefense.org/child-research-data-publications/data/2014-soac.pdf?utm_source=2014-SOAC-PDF&utm_medium=link&utm_campaign=2014-SOAC.
10 Michaela W. Columbo, "Reflections from Teachers of Culturally Diverse Children," *Beyond the Journal: Young Children on the Web*, National Association for the Education of Young Children (November 2005): 2, http://www.naeyc.org/files/yc/file/200511/ColomboBTJ1105.pdf.
11 Sonia Nieto and Patty Bode, *Affirming Diversity: Sociopolitical Context of Multicultural Education*, 6th ed. (Boston: Pearson, 2012), 32-34.
12 For an example of such a process, see Chip Wood and Babs Freeman-Loftis, "Chapter One: Seven Key Leadership Actions," in *Responsive School Discipline: Essentials for Elementary School Leaders* (Turners Falls, MA: Northeast Foundation for Children, 2011), 11-21.
13 Personal correspondence, Paul Carolan, RMMS Director, February, 2014. See also Acknowledgments.
14 Donald R. Moore and Gail Merritt, *Chicago's Local School Councils: What the Research Says* (Chicago: Designs for Change, 2002), 9-11.
15 David L. Kirp, *Improbable Scholars: Rebirth of a Great American School System and a Strategy for America's Schools* (New York: Oxford University Press, 2013), 9, 15, 62.
16 Iowa City Community School District, Weber Elementary job listing, "Student and Family Advocate Elementary, Weber," http://k12jobspot.com/jobs/?ID=558917.
17 Shoreline School District Family Advocacy Department, Shoreline Public Schools, "What Can Your Family Advocate Do for You?" (2012): 2, http://schools.shoreline-schools.org/studentservices/files/2011/05/Family-Advocate-Brochure2.pdf.
18 Other districts listing school family advocates in 2014 (as accessed on the Internet 2/27/2014) include Sacramento, CA, Amphitheater Public Schools, Tucson, AZ, Jefferson County, MO, Irvington, NJ, and Apple Valley, MN.
19 As late as 1965 the creation of certified training and employment for nurse practitioners was nothing but an act of imagination and hope voiced by practitioners and leaders in the field of health care and medicine. Of note, the first nurse practitioners were pediatric nurses. By the late 60's early 70's, graduate programs for nurse practitioners were established at University of Colorado, Boston College, University of Washington, and elsewhere. In 1980, the position of Family Nurse Practitioner was added to some ten other categories such as Oncology Nurse Practitioner, etc. By 2014 there were 189,000 nurse practitioners represented by a national organization, and more nationwide. Today, most individuals and families have met a nurse practitioner and accept their role and expertise in helping them with their health care.
20 Rebecca Onie, "What If Our Health Care System Kept Us Healthy?" hosted by Guy Raz, *TED Radio Hour* (March 14, 2014), http://www.npr.org/templates/transcript/transcript.php?storyId=288689497. See also Healthleadsusa.org.

CHAPTER THREE

Personalized Learning

Children are more likely to see value in formal learning, put energy into it, and increase their skills and knowledge when school experiences are personalized enough to meet their fundamental needs: relationship; a safe, inclusive community; a sense of competence and autonomy; and some fun now and then. How can we address these needs as we work to build skills with individual children and with small groups?

RELATIONSHIP: Children do better when their teachers know them well personally, developmentally, and culturally, and we demonstrate this knowledge. They do better when we show that we care about them and are available for them academically, emotionally, and socially. They know we care and can sense our connection to them through verbal and nonverbal cues we give them: we are attuned to each other. They do better when we hold a growth mindset—we believe in their capacity to grow and succeed. "This growth mindset is based on the belief that your basic qualities are things that you can cultivate through your efforts. Although people may differ in every which way—in their initial talents and aptitudes, interests, or temperaments—everyone can change and grow through application and experience."[1]

COMMUNITY: Children do better when we provide an orderly and safe community so the energy and focus of each child is not diminished by distraction, irritation, or loss of control. They do better when we establish and maintain structures and routines that are inclusive and equitable, so each child's commitment to learning is not diminished by loneliness, frustration, or anxiety.

COMPETENCE: Children do better when we share with them accurate information about the skills and knowledge they have, and we plan for future growth together. We decide together whether and when a student is ready for the introduction of new skills and knowledge, so s/he can grow from success to success, and we confirm their growing competence by sharing accurate assessments of continuing progress. We understand the crucial importance of the child's being aware of his or her progress in order to sustain a growth mindset, a belief that effort will bring proficiency.

AUTONOMY: Children do better when we challenge them to take a leading role in their own development: setting goals, making choices about how to achieve those goals, and then assessing growth. They do better when we maintain a relationship of mutual respect and reciprocity in our journey together of teaching and learning.

PLAY: Children do better when we notice and enjoy light moments, perhaps moments of playfulness, that add pleasure and energy to the work of education. They do better when we take time for a quick game or move a bit or sing a song together to lighten the mood.

Creating "real teaching"

I was talking with a teacher about how the school day had gone. She said it had been great, one of the best days she'd had. "Today," she said, "I did *real* teaching." I asked what she meant by "real" teaching, and she said, "I worked a lot with individual children, helping each one wherever they were—a stuck place, excited about a new project, heading the wrong way on an assignment, or frustrated over a drawing. I could step in wherever a child was at the moment and help him or her move forward. And they did—all of them!"

She was generating personalized learning. She was a partner with each student as s/he moved along the learning route from first exposure to skill or content, to attempting the skill or reaching for the understanding but needing help, to the end point, when the child is able to handle the skill or apply the knowledge independently. Developmental psychologist Lev Vygotsky called the "needing help" stage the zone of proximal development, or the ZPD. He described it as the area of learning that is close to emergence in a child and will emerge in collaboration with the teacher or another child.[2] In my friend's classroom, the students experienced success and growth. Every student made progress, and everyone—children and teacher alike—knew it.

Of course students are most likely to move from success to success when the learning is orchestrated just right for each one. And without steady growth, when academic demands seem to exceed their reach, of course they get discouraged and begin to lose belief in their capacity to learn—sometimes even their teachers begin to lose faith. Personalized learning through *Elementary Designs* practices offers the opportunities students need every day to engage in learning within their reach. In this chapter, we focus on personalized learning with individuals and small groups that keeps all learners—the ones we're working with at a particular moment, as well as the rest of the class—engaged and on a growth trajectory. Chapter Five provides further support for fostering the student self-management and independence necessary for a personalized learning environment.

Personalized Learning Examples

What makes teaching and learning personal is effectively addressing the needs of each learner. Content, delivery, response, and assessment all take into account both universal human needs and the needs of the particular child at this moment in his or her life, developmentally, culturally, and personally.

Jaylin

Jaylin is a nine-year-old African-American boy who struggles to read. He is sociable, interested in having books read to him, and embarrassed to be a non-reader in third grade. His family has been homeless for many months and finally found temporary housing through a charitable organization. His mom and three brothers are living in a small apartment while the agency looks for permanent housing for them. Jaylin receives special education services at school, as well as tutoring, but progress is slow. Whenever he doesn't know a word or can't sound a letter, he pounds the table and tosses his head in what might be frustration, but seems more like an attempt to push the whole process away.

What does personalized learning for Jaylin look like? It begins with partnership. Promising Jaylin steadfast support in learning to read, and asking him if he is willing to work at it, are the first steps. And the work needs to include some fun—joking about the silly stories in the books at the beginner's level, playing reading games together, laughing about nonsense words. It helps to use manipulatives, so Jaylin can work with his hands to assemble words. Active learning suits his energy and his nervousness regarding the task before him. Making choices about which phoneme to work on, which book to read, or which manipulative to use gives him some control of the process, providing him some dignity. His teachers employ all of these tactics. Slowly, resistance drops away, and Jaylin accumulates sight words and phonemes he can recognize. One day he reads a book at the "A" level, and he is happy to experience growth.

Personalized learning for Jaylin means establishing relationships with him that he can trust and enjoy. His teachers have to get to know him, learn about his home life, find out what he enjoys, and present work in ways that appeal to him. It means finding books that interest him, and talking about the content together. Personalizing his learning means sharing the process of assessment and acknowledging each success so the all-too-familiar stuck feeling doesn't return. His teachers need to share with Jaylin about being scared sometimes, about what is fun for them, and what makes them nervous sometimes. In short, his teachers have to build relationship with him as two people sharing a bit of life. In those relationships, self-respect and trust can grow, providing an environment in which Jaylin can muster the courage to do hard work.

Psychologists and researchers Bridgett Harme and Robert Pianta followed a group of kindergartners through eighth grade. They found that the quality of the teacher-student relationship in kindergarten predicted a number of academic and behavioral outcomes in eighth grade, especially for students who had many behavior problems. They write, "Forming strong and supportive relationships with teachers allows students to feel safer and more secure in the school setting, feel more competent, make more positive connections with peers, and make greater academic gains." Teachers connect with their students by showing and telling them: "I am interested in you... I accept you.... Adults can be helpers... I am consistent... I am safe... You have competencies... I will be here even when things get tough....I can read your signals and will respond to them...."[3]

David

David is a sunny European-American first grader with lots of friends. His parents have high school diplomas and work at low-paying jobs; money is short in David's home. He changed schools after kindergarten, and might have to change again if his family has to find other housing. He is on the free and reduced-price lunch list, and when asked why he was glad to be back at school after the winter break, David said, "Because we get breakfast every day!"

David finds schoolwork pretty hard, and his progress in early word work is slow. In mid-November he was stuck on learning the consonant blend "cr" at the beginning of words. He just couldn't seem to remember it, despite a lesson with his teacher. One day his teacher sat beside him and they took it on one more time, thinking of words beginning with "cr." This time David could hear the sound well enough to find words that used it, so he said each word and his teacher wrote it on the list. Then it was time to read back the words on the list. David began with the first few words he was able to read. Then he came to "crap."

"What's that?" he said.

"Crap," his teacher replied, "It's not a word we use in school, but you said it, so I wrote it down."

"I didn't say *crap*! I said *crack*," David exclaimed.

"Uh oh," his teacher replied with a wink. "Don't tell anyone I made *that* mistake!"

Two children nearby heard the conversation and soon everyone was laughing. David was gleeful at the "secret," and when it was time to read the whole list again, he did so—every word just right, smiling the whole time.

A couple of months later, after winter break, David was checking in with his teacher. By then he could read six consonant blends. He read his list of words to his teacher, beginning with the consonant blends he knew, then coupling them with the vowel sounds he knew, and got them all right. "You're ready to move on, David! Nice going!" the teacher said. David smiled, "Yeah, but remember that 'cr' time! It was so great that I could read that whole card full of 'cr' words!" The "cr" moment was a highlight for David.

Months later, he was still moving from success to success. Was it the laughter he remembered? Was it catching the teacher in a mistake? Was it the fact that "crap" was not a "school" word? What experiences may have made learning to read seem more attainable for a boy who was struggling? Reading still doesn't come easily for David, but he has no resistance to it, and he knows he can learn. After all, "Remember that "cr" time!"

Relationships with students are based on knowing them

Relationship was established for Jaylin and David as they became well known to their teachers developmentally, culturally, and personally. Jaylin's teachers know that Jaylin, who just turned nine, is at a typically somewhat insecure stage of development, moving toward adolescence, but still a child, anxious about what might go wrong and about taking risks in a world that seems basically unfair. Many nine-year-olds easily take offense, and criticism and failure can be devastating. Jaylin's teachers know he and his family are having hard times. Like many nine-year-olds, he is self-critical, and his failure to read is near the top of the list of things he feels bad about. Encouragement, a firm belief in his possibilities for growth—these supports are crucial for Jaylin.

Culturally, Jaylin lives in generational poverty. His mother struggles to support herself and her four boys, and she has little hope that things might change. She and her children have no supportive community except the shelter staff. Without a high school diploma, she is unlikely to find work that can support them. She and the boys have some fun times together, but they live with chronic insecurity and fear of the future. The times when Jaylin's classmates play a game together or when he and a teacher have a laugh are highlights in his life. He even has moments when his teacher's belief in his growth rubs off on him and he begins to hope.

On the other hand, David's life at home is secure. His parents take an interest in what David is doing and try to support his learning, but they have little time to read aloud or help with homework. They find a way for at least one of them to be at school conferences, and they make sure David gets to school on time. Culturally, the family has no resources for travel or visits to museums, but their home is stable. There are no books around, and the television is on almost all the time.

David's parents are optimistic about providing for their family. His dad is going to school at night for automotive technical training, and he hopes to get a job that pays better. Personally, David is tidy and careful. He seems happy most of the time, is willing to work hard, and enjoys partnering with his teacher for his growth. He likes to make decisions about when to "move on" to another phoneme or word list, and does so only after reading all the ones he has been assigned "two times, just right." (Read more about when students "move on" below on page 83.)

Competence, autonomy, community, and play emerge from relationship

Jaylin and David's learning occurs in the context of connection between the teacher and the child. In this fertile soil, the other elementary requirements of teaching for equity can thrive:

- **COMPETENCY:** Jaylin and David's learning is designed as often as possible around each child's skill level, interests, and learning preferences. They move from success to success, however small the steps, and experience themselves as growing in competence and autonomy.
- **AUTONOMY:** Jaylin and David both have opportunities to manage parts of their school days, and their teachers invite and listen to their ideas with interest.
- **COMMUNITY:** For both boys, learning occurs within a safe, inclusive community that reflects and responds to the lives of the students—their cultures, their families, their interests, their strengths, and their feelings.

- **PLAY:** Both boys experience some moments of pleasure and fun in school every day.

The Basics of Personalized Learning

Personalized learning can happen when we work one-to-one with students, but also in a whole-class setting, between partners, in small groups, and when a student is working alone (see Chapter Four for a discussion of personalized learning with the whole group). It depends on knowing our students' interests, strengths, cultural backgrounds, preferences, and levels of skill. It requires that we design learning experiences that engage students at the right levels, and with the content (insofar as we can control it) and ways of learning that are meaningful to them.

To accomplish this, there is nothing more important than the relationships we build with students. Even when it is a stretch to match the curriculum with what we know of students, and we fall short of a perfect match, the effort to get to know them and to design the learning around them is not wasted. It can make all the difference for their success.

Relationship is the foundation

Your relationship with any particular student is specific to the two of you. Besides involving what you know about the child, his family, his culture, his preferences and habits, and also what he knows of you, it is also shaped by the qualities of your exchanges each day. Do you laugh together? Do you look at each other when you interact? Who does most of the talking? (Allowing him or her to help make some decisions, share ideas, and offer examples relevant to his or her own life adjusts the power differential of the student-teacher relationship and increases our attunement.) Are you responsive to his needs—cognitive, emotional, and social? If so, the learning will take hold. See Chapter One, page 15, for a definition of and research basis for attunement.

"Each child is unique. The attuned teacher becomes an historian, remembering and cataloguing a child's style of engagement and communication."[4]

Knowing and appreciating each child and building learning for and around each one are major tasks. To come to know twenty or thirty individuals well enough to help each one to be willing and able to learn requires that we seek out information from and establish helpful connections with home and neighborhood, and that we constantly watch and listen for telling clues—the averted eyes, the sagging shoulders, relaxation after laughter. With attunement, there is a constant stream of information between teacher and students.

A student profile for Luann

The more a teacher knows about a student, the more effectively s/he can help her or him. Why does Luann jump into the spotlight whenever she gets a chance? Why does she say she knows the answer to a question and then just giggle when I ask her to share her answer? Why does she scan the room instead of keeping her eyes on the page when she reads to me? The more I know about her, the better I can meet her need for relationship, and the better I can guide her toward the competence and independence she wants and needs.

One way I can organize my thinking to reveal patterns of behavior is to create a profile for Luann, a description of her from multiple points of view. What do I know about her developmentally? How does she compare to the average eight-year-old? Is she always in a hurry when she does things? Does she love to socialize? Is she always wanting to talk? Developmentally, Luann seems typical for her age.

What do I know about her home life? Her dad has a job in a shipping department and her mom is a cook in a café. Both are artists—he plays guitar in a small band and she is a painter. The schedule at home is erratic because her mom has to work at night sometimes, and her dad plays evenings when his band gets a gig. Luann and her brother are on their own a lot.

Personally, Luann has lots of friends, but recently I've noticed that some of the girls get mad at her for what they describe as her "bossiness." She seems uninterested in reading or doing her math homework, but she'll spend half an hour on a drawing, getting each part "just right." That's about the only time she is quiet and focused for an extended time. She ignores or is unaware of boundaries of both space and time, and she needs multiple redirections every day. She retains her good humor, however, and always tells me she'll do better. She is not where she needs to be in reading, writing, or math.

STUDENT PROFILE EXAMPLE

See blank profile form in Resources, page 171.

Name: Luann

Assets profile: She has a lot to say and is articulate. She could be a good writer. She often talks over other children—she always has an opinion and tends to dominate conversations, but most of the time her opinions make sense, and with some coaching, she could become a strong leader. Unfocused (she often doesn't focus on what I want her to), but when she's interested, she's like a laser and highly motivated. Strong willed and breaks rules: she has her own ideas and the will to carry them out. If I could help her channel that energy into constructive projects, she could produce wonderful work. She loves to sing and has a beautiful voice.

Developmental profile: Physically healthy, average size for an eight-year-old; more skilled with small-motor than large-motor movement; has fun with friends at recess and is included in work groups, especially if the task involves drawing. Luann seems to be a concrete thinker most of the time, and is not comfortable with abstractions. She does much better in math when she can use manipulatives.

Preferred learning mode: She strongly prefers the visual and kinesthetic over the auditory. She's dominant in group work or on the playground, unless it involves a lot of math, where she lacks confidence.

Personal/cultural profile: Parents are artists (musical and visual); home schedule varies because of parents' work and performance schedules. Luann and her ten-year-old brother are on their own for part of most days. They are expected to help with chores.

Needs profile: Good friends with Maria (when they aren't having a disagreement); seems to like and have fun with everyone, but some shy away from her strong personality; is making progress in reading, writing, math; needs opportunities to create and lead productively.

What could I do and say to support her growth? I could structure opportunities for Luann to lead, such as acting out a story with a small group, scaffolding her to success by providing a format for a written script and helping her get started. I could channel her drawing into writing by introducing her to cartoon-making with dialogue for cartoon characters.

Good-Better-Best talk

After thinking hard about a child, gathering information about her from the family, observing and listening in class and elsewhere, and examining her work products, you are ready to have a one-to-one Good-Better-Best talk with her. The objective of the conversation is to acknowledge what is going well, identify what could be better, and strategize for the best possible school experience and outcomes. The talk should take five to ten minutes, and the questions are designed to both learn more about how the student sees her school life and to strategize together on how to optimize it. We can ask questions such as:

- How do you feel at school? (Help with "I've noticed" statements: "I've noticed you jump rope with others or alone at recess, and I've noticed that sometimes you look sad.")
- What do you enjoy in school? ("I've noticed that you almost always volunteer to run errands for me;" "I've noticed that you check books out of the library every week.")
- What is hard for you? (Help by asking "Could it be...." Questions: "Could it be that this math skill is still as hard for you as it was at the beginning of the year?")
- How can we make what is hard easier? (Suggest projects or variations on assignments or ways the child can get help: "Would you like an eighth grader to help you in math once a week?")
- How will you get started? (As soon as possible, establish some momentum by getting the student started on something that will enhance her school experience.)

Leave room for the child to do as much of the talking as possible. Keep your focus on her or him and any indications of a shift in attitude or strong feelings—body language, teary eyes, nervous shuffling, etc. Your observations will tell you whether to go on talking or to let a little silence occur between you. Allowing some silence will help you discern what is going on, how the child feels, whether s/he is open to change.

Sample Good-Better-Best talk with Luann

I need to connect with Luann. During partner reading time, I'll ask her for a ten-minute conference designed to improve her school experience. I'll listen carefully to her description of what her school day is like, and then we'll figure out at least one way she can have more success—and more fun—in school every day. Here's how our talk might go:

Me: *Luann, how is your time at school these day? Do you have fun? Are you learning a lot?*

Luann: *I have fun sometimes, but I wish it was more fun. I wish we had more recess and more time for art. I like to draw, but I don't like to read or do math, because I'm not good at those. I'm not good at school stuff, but I'm good at drawing.*

Me: *I know what you mean. I'm good at making pies, and it makes me happy to make five different kinds of pies and have people enjoy them. I also like being your teacher and knowing that by the end of the year, you will be reading and enjoying books! I have an idea you might like: you could write your own book and illustrate it, and then you could read it and show it to other people. If the book were appropriate, you could even read it to the kindergartners. Would that be fun?*

Luann: *Sure.*

Me: *Let's think up something you are good at making or doing. We could write about that.*

Luann: *I'm good at drawing, and I'm great at making sandwiches. My mom says they're Dagwood sandwiches because they're huge, with everything in the refrigerator in them.*

Me: *I didn't know that about you. Would you like to write and illustrate a book on how to make a Dagwood sandwich?*

Luann: *I don't know how to write a book.*

Me: *I'll help. Let's start with you dictating the instructions to me and I'll write them down. Dictating means you say the words out loud and I write them. So what should the title page say?*

Luann: *How to Make a Dagwood Sandwich.*

Me: *OK, I've written it down. Now you copy it onto the cover of this blank book I made for you, and make the letters look nice, like a book cover.* (Luann copies *How to Make a Dagwood Sandwich*)

We'll continue with Luann dictating the steps, while I write them down. When the sandwich is "made," I'll send Luann off with the words on the pages of the little book and plenty of room for illustrations of the steps of the process. She is excited and comes back to the work eagerly after gym. Later I will ask her to read her book to me, perhaps to the class, if she is willing, and perhaps to the kindergartners.

Incremental success and mastery for Luann

The progress needs to be continuous. Once a student has mastered a skill or some content and our assessment indicates that s/he can operate solo in that endeavor, s/he moves on. My next question for Luann, for example, is "Would you like to be able to write down your own words?" Continuous progress is the model, accompanied by assessment, with ever-increasing competence and autonomy the goal. All this needs to happen in the context of a knowing relationship, a caring community around us, and the spice of some fun.

How does the teacher decide what needs to be taught when and to whom? Some (not many) teachers are invited to design their own curriculum based on the needs and interests of their students; some have both curriculum and instruction prescribed for them. Most do their own planning, but must base that planning on a set of standards for each subject.

I started with the standards and benchmarks for my grade levels and then put together a comprehensive list of vowel and consonant combinations. For example, for Minnesota Language Arts standard #7 for first grade (Generate rhyming words in a rhyming pattern) I compiled a list of word "families," such as the "at," "an," "in," and "it" families. Students choose which family to work on in what order, but in the end, they will have mastered these sound combinations and the concept of rhyming. When a child masters a skill, she and I plan together which skill she will work on next. (First/second grade teacher)

See Resources, pages 177-179, for examples of reading growth records this teacher and her students use. The goal, as always in personalized learning, is that each child progresses at his/her own personalized rate and knows s/he is progressing steadily.

Personalized learning provides a path to proficiency

Personalized learning avoids whole-class instruction in skill-building areas in which individual students vary in their competencies. It also avoids the deficit model of remedial work for those who can't keep up with a whole-class lesson (because those lessons were not appropriate for them in the first place), and everyone grows from success to success. If a child needs extra lessons, s/he participates in one or more one-to-one personalized learning session(s) with the teacher, or in a small group learning the same skill or content. We cannot teach from the front of the room to all learners in the class at once. For a particular skill or understanding, students are often in various places of development, so we aim our instruction to avoid simply "covering the material," and instead teach for proficiency and for equity.

Structure for Personalized Learning

Above all, personalized learning is a partnership. Children work in small groups or individually with the teacher or another adult for support in developing a skill. When they can perform the skill on their own, they practice it until they demonstrate proficiency. The process is a somewhat spiraling cycle in which communication may be enhanced by collaboration, verbal and nonverbal mediators, manipulatives, and games.

- **FORMATIVE ASSESSMENT FOR GOAL SETTING:** With the student, assess his or her proficiency in a skill. Collaborate with the student to set a just-right goal (something that s/he can do with assistance, but not yet independently). Offer choices if more than one goal could be appropriate.

- **SCAFFOLD PRACTICE:** Throughout the student's process of developing the skill, note the spots where s/he has difficulty, and provide verbal support and nonverbal mediators, like a reminder card or movable letters, hand signals, or something she can do or say to herself to support her success (for example, distinguish "b and d" by clarifying them kinesthetically, making the two letters with your fingers, or provide beads or other counters to work with sums or differences).

- **GROWTH RECOGNITION:** When a student can perform a skill without adult help (although still with the help of mediators, if needed), s/he is ready to work independently. Together, you decide when s/he has achieved that level of skill. Record the progress in your records and in the child's folder, and enjoy the moment. You might want to send a note home informing the family of their child's success (see pages 42 and 85 for a description of Yes! cards).

- **INDEPENDENT OR PEER PRACTICE:** Provide students ways to practice a skill, such as a game that requires it, or a problem sheet, or dice or letters to make up her own challenges and record them. To practice effectively, s/he needs a way to control for errors, such as an answer sheet, manipulatives to check an answer, or a partner who can act as a checker,

- **FORMATIVE ASSESSMENT FOR NEXT STEPS:** Check in again by reviewing the student's practice work or by observing the practice in progress, or by having the student demonstrate the skill the next time she works with you one-to-one or in a small group. If she can do it proficiently, she is ready to move on to another skill.

Brianna's Personalized Learning Lesson

Here is first grader Brianna, who is learning sound-symbol correspondence as it applies to consonant blends. Brianna's goal for this school year is to read chapter books. She gets plenty of school support from her parents. Her mom works part time, and she and Brianna visit the library almost every week. They read together every night, and Brianna is beginning to pick out some of the words herself. Her favorite books are the ones she calls "tricky," stories that have characters who deal with complicated situations. Brianna is impatient with word work—decoding the consonant blends, vowels, and word families. She wants to hurry on to "real" reading.

Brianna and her teacher establish the goal together

"Brianna, since we agree that you've got that 'pl' beginning for words, it's time to move on. Let's try another blend of two consonants. Here's the list—pick one." Brianna sighs and points to "st." "This one."

An important part of the work that Brianna and her teacher do together is assessing which skills she has mastered and which ones need more work. They work together on the assessment. Together they come to the conclusion that Brianna has achieved proficiency in a certain skill and no longer needs help sounding out those words or vowel-consonant combinations. In Brianna's class, that's called being ready to move on. They are good at determining the right moment, but they look to the teacher for confirmation. They count up the number of times they read a word correctly to decide if it's in their "got it!" stack, but they also count on their teacher to watch and listen carefully. Their relationship is built on trust: they are all on the same side, and if there is a reason for Brianna to not move on, she knows that her teacher will tell her. The assessment process is formative—that is, it has one purpose: to help them form a plan for their next step, one step after another, success after success. Together they make the assessment, and together they take pleasure in Brianna's accomplishment.

Student practice with the teacher

"Let's see how many words you can think of that begin with the 'st' sound." Brianna works with a list of words that start with "st," but she also gets to generate words of her own. She likes that. Some of her words are funny: she says, "stupid!" and she and the teacher laugh. The teacher says, "start," Brianna says, "stop!" and they go on, the teacher printing them in a list.

Some of the words Brianna generates are nonsense words that she and her teacher have to figure out how to spell, but nonetheless, they begin with the "st" sound, so they put them on the list (with "Ha-ha!" next to them to indicate that they are jokes). It's fun, but Brianna knows it's work, too, and she is proud, even though she wants to really read.

A mediator to support practice

"Say the 'st,' then add a vowel sound, like 'st' and the long 'a' sound as in "stay." See if any words occur to you."

Brianna can talk herself through the consonant-vowel combination to figure out a word. This self-talk mediates the task. It takes the place of the teacher helping her by giving her a way she can help herself. "Have children talk when you want them to process new information or solidify old information."[5]

"Now let's see if you can read back all those 'st' words we said. Remember that each word begins with the 'st' sound, so say that, then the vowel that follows, and so on." The teacher guides Brianna steadily toward success.

Concrete materials as mediators

An example of a concrete mediator is word cards that contain all but the "st" in words that begin with that letter combination. Brianna's job is to add the starting sound in front of the partial words. Her teacher tells her: "Here is a list of sounds ('ay' 'ack,' 'art,' 'em'). Put the 'st' card at the beginning of them and read the word that's formed." Once again, Brianna is learning with some help, and the help is not directly from the teacher to her, but from a tangible aid that the teacher gave her as a mediator between Brianna and the skill she is learning.

Brianna's teacher may provide magnetic letters that Brianna can use to set up the phoneme "an" on a board, and slide different letters in front of it to see what words she can make, then check those words against her 'an' word family card. These supports create a scaffold for Brianna to practice until she no longer needs their help, and can read and write words in the "an" family correctly and independently. More success!

A good teacher, like a good builder, provides the scaffold that makes it possible for each of the children to move from dependence to independence, competence, and confidence. At that point, the scaffold can be removed, "showing off walls of sure and solid stone."[6]

Reciprocal assessment

Brianna reads the words she has created and the ones she and her teacher brainstormed, then thinks of a few more, which the teacher adds to the list. The lesson is almost over, and together Brianna and her teacher discuss Brianna's achievement. They are satisfied that Brianna can now work on "st" words on her own, another step toward reading mastery.

Independent practice

The teacher gives Brianna a list to read for practice, and encourages her to add to it if she thinks of additional "st "words. Brianna joins the other children who are working on their reading skills at various tables or stations, and she practices for ten or fifteen minutes. She checks her work with a teacher-designated partner (a child who has mastered the "st" phoneme) to make sure she reads the words correctly. If she has missed some, Brianna can practice a little more until finally she decides she is ready to move on. She will check with her teacher for agreement.

Incremental growth, step by step

The next day, Brianna and a few other students who have also been working on initial consonant blends meet with the teacher to add a new blend to the list of initial phonemes they can read. The teacher starts the mini-lesson off with a review. "Brianna, will you read to the group the list of 'st' words you studied yesterday?" Brianna reads the list to the group. She exchanges a satisfied look with her teacher (attunement!). This is a "moving on" moment, and it reaffirms Brianna's confidence that she is making progress. The teacher notes in her record that Brianna can read most words that begin with "st" and checks off "st" in the list of phonemes in Brianna's reading folder, indicating that she is ready to move on to other initial consonant blends. One by one, she will master consonant blends, sight words, families of rhyming words, and she will soon be *really* reading! She will have matching cards, sorting trays, and other active-learning materials to provide variety in her independent learning, make it more fun, and keep her engaged. Her teacher is providing the scaffold that Brianna can climb to become a fluent reader.

The moving on moments are delicious. They announce to the student that he or she is successfully learning, and they promise new challenge. They build the student's can-do attitude that leads to success in school. They affirm for the teacher that she is doing well, meeting student needs and guiding them on. Later in the year—especially if she notices Brianna stumbling when she reads aloud—the teacher may return to some of the tricky "st" words to reinforce Brianna's learning and continue to move her toward mastery. Spiraling back, then moving forward again, has helped Brianna become confident in her growth. She works at reading because she sees value in it for herself, and her expectation is that she will get better and better. She expects that she will be reading as well as her older brother some day! Her teacher delights in her growth mindset.

With a high value placed on learning to read and high expectations that she will learn how to read well, Brianna makes steady progress:

"Youngsters may greatly value the idea of improving their reading. They usually are not happy with limited skills and know they would feel a lot better about if they could read. But often they experience everything the teacher asks them to do as a waste of time. They have done it all before, and they still have a reading problem.

"...High expectations paired with low valuing also yield low approach motivation. Thus, the oft cited remedial strategy of guaranteeing success by designing tasks to be very easy is not as simple a recipe as it sounds. Indeed, the approach is likely to fail if the outcome (e.g., improved reading, learning math fundamentals, applying social skills) is not valued or if the tasks are experienced as too boring or if doing them is seen as too embarrassing. In such cases, a strong negative value is attached to the activities, and this contributes to avoidance motivation."[7]

"Two common reasons people give for not bothering to learn something are 'It's not worth it' and 'I know I won't be able to do it.' In general, the amount of time and energy spent on an activity seems dependent on how much it is valued by the person and on the person's expectation that what is valued will be attained without too great a cost." [8]

Check-ins and record-keeping

Brianna's teacher keeps track of Brianna's progress in reading and math skills. She has a notebook for each subject with a section for each student. She keeps a record of the skills the student has been introduced to and has spent time practicing with mediators, and notes when the student achieves a level of proficiency and is ready to move on to other skills. See Resources, pages 177-179, for record-keeping examples.

Brianna's teacher keeps a less detailed record of Brianna's accomplishments in Brianna's reading and math folders where Brianna can refer to them. In meetings with Brianna, the teacher can review with her all she has accomplished to date. At these sessions she may catch up on Brianna's home life and her current interests, and hear any concerns she may have. They review Brianna's progress, note what she can do independently, and plan together (with some choices for Brianna to make) the challenges she will take on now. The teacher continues to cultivate Brianna's growth mindset and acknowledges her hard work and success. She closes the loop by preparing a "Yes!" card for Brianna's family, noting her progress in what she can now do on her own (her independent skills) and/or the new things she can do with some help (her emerging skills). See Chapter Two, page 42, for other content possibilities for Yes! cards and Resources, page 176, for a sample.

This model of personalized learning is designed to be used with all students of all skill levels. Brianna is attaining her reading skills more slowly than many of her classmates, and faster than some, but such comparisons rarely occur in her class, because all the students are progressing on their individual paths. She knows she is succeeding, step by step.

Knowing Families Makes Learning Personal

Teaching children one by one or in small groups is a personal experience for both the children and their teacher. We don't work with Brianna exactly the same way we work with Jaylin or David or Luann. Life is different for each of them, so their interests and understandings are different. With Jaylin, the teacher chats about football and checks to make sure he's had enough to eat today. She watches a boy as he arrives in the morning to see whether he seems more somber than usual, because she knows his mother is ill. Another needs to share with her teacher about her new kitten before they get down to work, or she will not be able to concentrate. The single most important thing we do as teachers is watch, listen to, and get to know every student.

To get to know children well, we must get to know and keep in touch with their families. We need to know about their lives outside of school, their cultures, and their neighborhoods. When the school and the family are partners, the student wins. Most of the time, the task of bridging with families is up to us. We need to observe, ask questions, listen carefully, and watch for opportunities to build trust with students and their families. This further empowers us to provide the right scaffolding for each child.

Self-knowledge and a Growth Mindset Make Learning Personal

We need to know ourselves well to effectively personalize learning for students. The mood and mindsets we bring to school each day are crucial to our success as teachers. We need to connect with each and every student, and since many of them come from cultures and lifestyles different from ours, we must become aware enough of our own points of view, moods, and vulnerabilities to bridge the gaps so students and their parents or guardians trust that they are in safe hands.

Perhaps most important to students' success is our own growth mindset. We must believe that every student wants to learn and is able to learn, wants to be a good person and to succeed—even when they won't admit it—and that we have the insight and stamina to guide them. A growth mindset is at least as important for teachers as for students. It is a career-long process of nurturing academic optimism in our personality and character. Our belief in every student's unlimited ability to learn shapes our perception of him or her, and it influences how students feel and behave and how they perform socially, emotionally, and academically. We use our power as teachers to either open up or shut down learning for our students. The foundation of our effectiveness is our attunement with every student: we nurture and maintain a relationship with each of them, a unique connection, personal, precious, and powerful.

Personalized Independent Work

Most teachers ask, "What are the other children doing while I'm working with one child or a small group? If there is an aide in the room, some students are working with him or her, but how can I keep the entire class working productively?"

Three useful means for fostering positive learning behavior are a high level of engagement in learning, strong teacher-student relationships, and building social skills through mediators and peer-to-peer regulation. While the teacher is working one-to-one or with small groups and the children are engaged in independent practice, the teacher's eyes and ears are always scanning and listening to maintain an orderly work period. She provides mediators to remind students in concrete ways. For example, a student with the job of "sound checker" may circulate occasionally with a sign indicating the agreed-upon level, to remind everyone to control volume.

The best control for order among the rest of the class is their engagement in their tasks. Using concrete materials such as magnetic letters or phoneme "dice" or wax-covered bendable wires to make letters, and drawing or working with objects like math manipulatives or pocket charts that engage their hands and their minds. They can work with partners, playing learning games and checking each other's work. Most important, they all work at levels where they experience growing in mastery. Chapters Four and Five further address whole-class activities and the management of routines.

Three kinds of tasks and ways of working that students can engage in individually or with partners without continuous support from an adult are reading and writing; skill practice; and project learning and follow-up work.

Personalizing reading and writing

Although in many elementary classrooms reading and writing take place in readers' and writers' workshops, additional reading or writing is always a productive way to spend school time. Many of the same protocols as those that structure readers' and writers' workshops apply at general work times, except that the teacher works with individuals and small groups on a variety of topics, not exclusively on reading or writing.

Personalizing skill practice

Children can work on their skill competencies autonomously. Once a child has gained the capacity to independently perform a particular skill, s/he is ready to practice that skill on his or her own to solidify proficiency and pick up speed.

Control of error

Much independent work requires materials that have a built-in control of error that tells the student whether s/he is performing the task correctly. For example, s/he may have an answer sheet s/he can use to check his or her work. S/he might use puzzle problems, where the answer to a problem or equation is cut apart from the problem in a jigsaw manner; when the answer is correct, the puzzle pieces fit together. At the primary level, counting objects such as buttons or beads can serve as a work check. The student adds the numbers on paper, writes down the answer, then counts out objects to see if they equal the written sum.[9]

Students may be "accountability partners" who check each other's answers. Whatever the method, it is important to control for error when children work on their own.

Engaged work with materials

Since most young learners are highly kinesthetic in the ways they learn, active independent work suits them well. And many manipulatives and games offer the added advantage of providing a control for error. Counting objects, place-value boxes, flash cards, magnetic letters, and the like attract and engage many a learner, satisfying the desire for physical activity while accomplishing a cognitive task. Between ages five and ten (and often beyond), children need and crave movement.[10] And movement links a somatic memory to a cognitive skill, placing it in the learner's working memory.

"Learning theorists have suggested for some time that children's' concepts evolve through direct interaction with the environment, and materials provide a vehicle through which this can happen. This message has been conveyed in a number of ways: Piaget (1971) suggested that concepts are formed by children through a reconstruction of reality, not through an imitation of it; Dewey (1938) argued for the provision of firsthand experiences in a child's educational program; Bruner (1960) indicated that knowing is a process, not a product; and Dienes (1969), whose work specifically relates to mathematics instruction, suggested that children need to build or construct their own concepts from within rather than having those concepts imposed upon them."[11]

The student may have a choice of materials s/he will use to practice. Satisfying the needs for competence, autonomy, and movement, we make it more likely that s/he will persevere in the task and grow in skill.

Games make learning fun

Many games provide accountable ways to practice skills with concrete materials. Many require ordinary materials and can be handmade if time is more abundant than purchasing power.

EXAMPLE MATH GAME (K-2): Partners learn to compare whole numbers using a deck of number cards with dots or pictures to represent numbers. Partners each draw a card; they compare the two numbers and declare which is greater. They check for accuracy by counting the number of dots or objects on the cards. The person with the card with the larger number wins the round. Each time someone wins, s/he tallies a mark. When time runs out, the one with more marks wins the game.

Variety and options help personalize learning

Arrange the classroom for work while you are with individuals or small groups or circulating around the room. Arrange stations for partners to play games, to work with concrete math, to read or write, and so on.

Students can use electronic or live games independent of teacher intervention, except, perhaps, for initial instructions and check-ins. As long as control of error is included so students do not reinforce their mistakes, independent practice can be an engaging and effective form of learning. Electronic games provide immediate feedback to students, and the teacher can access a student's progress at any time or look at the whole class record. There are both concrete and electronic ready-made materials with built-in accuracy checks for dozens of K-5 skills.

Scaffolding for personal gains through partner work

Cognitive leverage occurs when students help one another independent of the teacher. They practice social skills like listening to one another, taking turns, observing each other carefully, and compromising, and they check each other to make sure work is correct. Their sense of competence grows as they help each other learn, and working together leverages their thinking and reinforces the skills of collaboration. Partners practice listening, sharing materials and time, and making room for others' perspectives. They practice explaining their points of view and reaching a solution, which may require integrating their thinking.

"The interaction of children who differ in age provides opportunities for leadership or emulation, whereas the interaction of peers of equal status allows for equality in the comparison and explanation of ideas. In addition, peer interaction may encourage an exploratory approach, with opportunities to examine and manipulate the rules of daily life in the imagination. And, not to be overlooked, peer interaction is motivating and available." [12]

Collaboration gives students feedback on their work, helping them assess their own performance more objectively. A partner, especially one who has mastered a skill and can perform it independently, can provide feedback on ideas and work performance. And with control for error, partners can learn together if they are at or near the same level. Students are more motivated to take on a task when they get to work with a peer. It might be fun, and can leverage efficiency: two or more people working on a task can divide the work, if necessary, to meet deadlines.

Partnering pitfalls

If one partner is more proficient than the other, s/he may take over or become impatient. If the partners are close friends, they may socialize more than strategize. Like all important skills, partnering must be learned. Rather than assume that students already know how to work with partners, we must teach them what productive collaboration looks, sounds, and feels like. See Chapter Four, page 136, for varied ways to form partnerships depending upon the outcomes you are seeking.

Demonstration and rehearsal

A good demonstration provides a memorable model to follow. For example, have a student do a demonstration with you (it's always more memorable when a peer is part of the demonstration) of working together, sharing ideas, and/or brainstorming. They might create a list of words or solve a math problem, using an answer sheet or a third person in the demo as a work checker. The work is primarily done in the partnership, but a checker could be conscripted when the work is complete. Or a triad of students can work together, taking turns being the checker.

To get the feel of collaborating and serving as a checker, students can try working with a partner on a problem or a reading or checking a partner's answers and listening to him or her read. Point out that sometimes it doesn't matter, but sometimes it is important that you partner with someone who already knows how to do the skill you are practicing so you can learn from her or him. The fact that students differ in their competencies at any particular time means that it is usually possible to pair more skilled with less skilled learners. (Again, we notice the importance of knowing your students well, so you can set up effective partnerships on the spot). At other times, an answer sheet (or list of word families or a spelling list) will be the "checker."

Listening

The teacher's guidance can help attune partners to one another: *Listen carefully to your partner. Instead of disagreeing or saying, "That's wrong," ask questions to understand your partner's point of view. And be sure to acknowledge a helpful contribution from your partner, or good work.*

For younger students: *Look at this color chart while your partner has her eyes closed, and describe one of the colors. When your partner opens her eyes and looks at the color, she can say whether it looks the way she expected it to from listening to you. Use your very best listening!*

Listening is essential for good partner work. Part of preparation for the work could be listening exercises such as:

- **LISTENING BY TURNS:** Student partners are given a topic to discuss; one takes the role of listener, one of speaker (use listener and speaker picture cards as mediators for younger children). Halfway through the process, they switch (cards and) roles.

- **TRIAD INTERMEDIATE LEVEL GROUPS DISCUSS AN ISSUE (E.G. HOW CAN WE MAKE CROSSING STREETS AS SAFE AS POSSIBLE?):** Two students listen silently while the third partner shares her opinion. Then the speaker and listeners change roles, then again, until all have expressed their ideas and all have listened to the others' ideas. Then the group discusses the ideas that all three have expressed.

- **PLAY A LISTENING GAME:** Students close their eyes, and you tell them, "listen carefully." They listen as you make a sound (ring a bell, shut a door, drop a pencil, etc.). Raising hands, students attempt to identify the sound. They will learn what you mean by "listen carefully." For older students, progress to more subtle sounds, like clapping the back of your hand or closing a book.

- **PLAY A LISTENING GAME WITH A SERIES OF DIRECTIONS:** Tell students to listen carefully, then give them a two-step direction, like "Put your hands on your ears and open your mouth." When they are successful, add more steps, like "stand on one foot, turn to your right, and clap your hands" or "touch your hair, touch your ears, touch your nose, and smile, in that order." Through these exercises, students develop memory and listening skills, and they get to move and have a little fun.

If students do not listen carefully to each other during partner work, the work is impaired. Interrupt, and either do another demonstration or repeat a listening game. If you notice that one person is dominating in some of the partnerships, stop the action and ask each group to give a one-minute summary of how their project or problem solving is going, then direct them to take turns speaking, one sentence at a time. This is somewhat artificial and stilted, but it forces more balance. For another exercise in listening carefully, direct partners to paraphrase what the other has said.

Reflecting on the partnership

When the work period is over, reinforce the importance of good partnering by reflecting on it:

- Did you and your partner share the work evenly?
- Did you help your partner? Did your partner help you?
- With a show of fingers in which five means you listened very carefully and zero or one means you didn't listen well at all, rate your listening.
- Indicate with your fingers the degree to which you felt listened to, five meaning "My partner listened carefully to everything I said."

See Resources, page 180, for a partner reflection form example.

Personalizing follow-up work

After a whole-class lesson, students can deepen their engagement and reinforce what they have learned by writing, making an observational drawing or a map, or other work that will deepen their understanding and help them remember what they have learned.

There is nothing like designing your own work to help you relate to it, to increase your investment and effort. What we invent, we own. The more opportunities we can give students to decide or help decide how and what they will do in school, the more school feels like a place where they belong. Allowing them to make some decisions about how they will learn gives them a personal stake in the outcome and makes the experience more meaningful. For example, after students have listened to a read-aloud and talked about a story together, they can read a book of their choice (level appropriate) and come back ready to share with the group something about the book.

The teacher says: *Decide how you will tell us or show us something about your book that will interest us in it and maybe make us want to read it. What are some ways we could share about our books?*

The children have ideas: *You could retell some of what you read. You could describe a character. You could draw a picture of one of the characters. You could make a story map. You could act out part of the story.*

The teacher records the list and posts it, and students start preparing their presentations for their audience. Options make it more likely that an assignment will engage everyone and tap various learning strengths.

Most ethnically diverse students [differing from European-American school culture] *find school boring and they often feel unwelcome, unimportant, and different, like they don't belong or fit in. What is taught has no immediate value to them, and they want something they can relate to, something that they recognize.* (Eleventh grade urban Hmong-American student)

Education theorist Gloria Ladson-Billings recognizes the value of more participatory and less lecture-dominated instruction: "Rather than the voice of one authority, meaning is made as a product of dialogue between and among individuals."[13]

Independent projects

To further increase students' investment in their learning, give them the chance to dig into learning something of particular interest to them over an extended period of time. Ideas for projects can come from a class field trip, from a speaker who gets students interested in a topic, or from a book. Everyone can start projects at the same time, or students can come up with their own project ideas during the year.

Project learning sparks engagement because it invites students to go deeper into something that interests them, and because at the end, it provides them an audience of their peers to see and listen to what they have learned and/or created. See below for descriptions of independent project processes and how to provide support.

Of the few memories I retain from my elementary school days, two that stand out were the time I made a relief map of the United States when we were studying geography, and the time I helped create a short play for the class to act out at our eighth grade graduation. In both cases, I was allowed to generate my own ideas and I got to move around, work with materials, and have an audience for my work. I was doing the things children like to do, and learning a lot at the same time. This is the big payoff in project work: it offers students time to generate rather than take in, to express themselves instead of absorbing someone else's ideas. New Zealand teacher and author Sylvia Ashton-Warner establishes a rhythm for the learning day that offers opportunities to "breathe out" (conversing, painting, creative writing, singing, learning words that are important to you, day dreaming, etc.) as well as "breathe in" (vocabulary building, learning your letters, reading, discussing, etc.).[14]

Projects make school more exciting. The effort to do one that you have thought up and designed yourself is not a struggle, especially if the teacher scaffolds your process so the project will be successful (see more about scaffolding below). The high level of engagement in project work accelerates achievement. It lights the fire that keeps the learner warm through the more proscribed learning of basic reading, writing, and math skills, and provides application ideas for those skills that make them seem important and worth learning.

Projects personalize learning by allowing students to choose a topic that is personally and culturally significant to them, and/or a way of learning that is attractive to them and suits their preferred mode (e.g., kinesthetic or visual, musical or verbal). A key factor in culturally responsive schooling is subject matter that is relevant, at least some of the time, to each child. Educator Maxine Greene writes, "If there is to be a truly humane, plague-free community in this country, it must be one responsive to increasing numbers of life-stories, to more and more 'different' voices."[15]

Independent project examples

A requirement in one school is that every fifth grader will do an independent project with a mentor. The students choose any topic that interests them, and they identify or are assigned an adult mentor who has interest in the topic (and in the child). With guidance and regular check-ins with the teacher, students research their topic. Sometimes the research involves a first-hand experience with a new skill or interviewing a person who has the skill or is knowledgeable about the topic. Students write a paper on their topic and make a presentation to an audience of their peers and their families. Engagement in these projects is very high, and school morphs, at least temporarily, from a "have-to" to a choice.

In another urban school, a first grade classroom studying "Our Neighborhood" takes a couple of walking field trips in which they get to know the businesses, artists, neighbors, and service people near their school. On a large table, they create a 3-D model of a two-block area around the school using pâpier-maché and other fun materials. Then partners select a business or person as their focus, and prepare a short description. Some of the neighbors visit the classroom and answer questions which were brainstormed ahead of time. Their answers become part of the map or the descriptions. At a culminating event, partners present the information they have gathered about a person or business, and the audience walks around the neighborhood map while the students offer more details they learned in their investigations. Engagement is very high during the neighborhood project, and it shows during the culminating presentation to the audience.

E4 format for project learning

We use "E4" to represent a format that project learning can follow:

Exploration

Individuals or partners investigate a topic of interest. This can happen after the class shares an experience together: an article or book, a video, a field trip, a guest speaker—any experience that introduces new knowledge or thinking can stimulate students to follow up with a project that digs deeper into the topic or looks at it from another point of view.

Expression

Individuals or partners develop and represent their understanding about the topic in an expressive form.

Exposition

Individuals or partners present their work to the group to communicate clearly what they have learned (see Chapter Four, page 132, for ways to development audience skills).

Evaluation

After the individuals or partners have presented their work, the group discusses the work, reflecting on points of interest, possible improvements, and/or places to go in order to continue the investigation of the topic.

Three cognitive skills crucial for high performance develop from this process of constructive learning followed by performance, reflection, and feedback:

- self-regulation: students organize work and persevere until completion
- application of deliberate memory: students use what they know, applying it to the project
- focused attention: students plan, execute their plan, present the product to others, then reflect on the process and product

These are skills that satisfy students' fundamental need for competence and autonomy by cultivating their capacity to think for themselves. In project learning, they are highly invested in the outcome, not merely because it is required, but also because the process is interesting, even enjoyable. Engage them, and they will learn!

E4 first/second grade study on animals ("critters")

- EXPLORATION: books on critters—each child/pair of partners reads about an animal
- EXPRESSION: each student or pair of partners represents the animal visually, dramatically, kinesthetically, or in a poem or story
- EXHIBITION: each student or pair of partners demonstrates or represents the animal to the group
- EVALUATION: each student or pair of partners and their audience reflects on the work, asking questions and/or suggesting a future follow-up activity; describing a strength of the presentation; and, if and when invited by the presenters, suggesting changes that might improve the work.

See Resources, page 172, for a detailed account of one teacher's whole-group lesson with project follow-up focused on immigration into the United States.

The power of independent projects

This is personalized learning at its most lively. Students learn about inquiring into a topic and about information-gathering. In other words, they get their first experience of research methodology. The process of investigation builds the crucial cognitive skills of focusing attention, deliberately applying what you remember, developing the determination it takes to resist the first or easiest answer and dig deeper, and building the vocabulary to express what you find. No wonder people who learn this way tend to become effective thinkers!

"Generally, research on project-based learning (PBL) has found that students who engage in this approach benefit from gains in factual learning that are equivalent or superior to those of students who engage in traditional forms of instruction (Thomas, 2000). The goals of PBL are broader, however, than simply the development of content knowledge. This approach aims to take learning one step further by enabling students to transfer their learning to new kinds of situations and problems and to use knowledge more proficiently in performance situations."[16]

Scaffolding personal project work

Just as an individual student needs teacher support and mediators to advance her or his learning of the basic skills of reading, writing, and math, all students need structure to support them when they are working on a project alone or with partners. That support can include learning to work with:

- a deadline that includes checkpoints for research, an outline, the first try, etc.
- a planning form that includes a list of steps to take and check off as progress is made toward the deadline date
- easily accessible source materials and Web addresses (specified and limited, for greater control of sources; more open for older students with experience in research)
- a strategy for solving problems along the way (e.g., use your best guess till you can check with someone; check an online source; ask another student; ask the teacher)
- scheduled check-ins with partners and weekly check-ins with the teacher
- reminder cards at computer stations to guide on-line researchers
- culminating performance for an audience
- a class- and teacher-constructed description of the characteristics of a quality project
- personal and group reflection on the projects using that description.

See a sample student planning form in Resources, page 174.

Technology partnerships in project learning

Partnerships collaborating on research increase efficiency and enhance learning. Partners can conduct their searches together at one computer station. Thus, in a social context for learning, cognitive skills—the 21st Century skills of critical thinking, perspective taking, and problem solving discussed in Chapter One—are put into action. In such an approach, the teacher can scaffold investigations by providing templates and rubrics as mediators to guide the work.

Audiences add meaning

Audiences for students' work can powerfully engage students in learning. Performance in the classroom need not be limited to showing one's work; students experience some of the power of performance when they lead their peers in a discussion, or when they address a group or even one person, especially if that person is the teacher. The more we allow students to share their work and to express themselves verbally, visually, musically, physically, or dramatically, the more we personalize their learning. Then they experience school as a place to be their authentic selves.

University of Illinois education Professor Arlette Ingram Willis raised the consciousness of many by telling the story of her African-American son's alienation from writing assignments in a school where he was in the minority among mostly European-American students: "I believe that Jake cannot bring this aspect of his life and culture into the classroom because he doesn't feel that it will be understood by his classmates and teacher. When Jake says 'They won't understand,' I interpret his words to mean that if his classmates cannot understand the simplest action in getting a haircut—the barber taking less than ten seconds to place a part in his hair—how can he expect them to understand the context and culture that surround the entire event.... It seems that he has come to understand that as an African American he must constantly make a mediating effort to help others understand events that appear to be commonplace on the surface, but are in fact culturally defined."[17]

We make the school experience relevant and meaningful to the great diversity of students we now encounter. Personalizing learning by tuning it to the reality of students' lives creates equal opportunities to learn. And learn they will, especially when their peers are listening and watching with interest.

Reflection and First Steps

Following is a list of elements of personalized learning described in this chapter. As you peruse the list and think back to what you have read, check the ones you think you are doing well, then identify an element that you feel is important to add to your teaching. Jot down some ideas for accomplishing that.

Ways to personalize learning in your classroom

1. Cultivate attuned teacher-student relationships
2. Scaffold student skill development
3. Meet children's needs for play and fun in learning
4. Know every student developmentally, culturally, and personally
5. Use a student profile to get to know students
6. Strategize for growth with a Good-Better-Best talk
7. Cultivate a growth mindset in yourself and in students
8. Scaffold for incremental success and proficiency
9. Set goals and assess work reciprocally with students
10. Use mediators to support learning
11. Support students' independent skill development with control of error
12. Scaffold growth through partner work
13. Recognize growth with "moving on" moments and progress records
14. Share growth news with Yes! cards for families
15. Include games, work centers, and manipulative materials for active skill development
16. Design activities to develop listening and reflecting skills
17. Personalize learning related to students' cultures, families, interests, strengths, and feelings
18. Plan and execute independent projects
19. Use the motivating power of audience

My reflection

1 Carol Dweck, *Mindset: New Psychology of Success: How We Can Learn to Fulfill our Potential* (New York: Random House, Ballantine, 2008), 7.

2 L.S. Vygotsky, "Thinking and Speech," *The Collected Works of L.S. Vygotsky, Volume 1: Problems of General Psychology*, ed. R.W. Rieber and A.S. Carton (New York: Plenum Press, 1987), 211.

3 Bridget K. Hamre and Robert C. Pianta, "Student-Teacher Relationships," *Children's Needs III: Development, Prevention, and Intervention*, ed. Kathleen M. Minke (Washington, DC: National Association of School Psychologists,2006), 56-57.

4 Bruce Perry, MD, PhD, "Attunement: Reading the Rhythms of the Child," *Teachers*, Scholastic.com http://www.scholastic.com/teachers/article/attunement-reading-rhythms-child.

5 Elena Bodrova and Deborah J. Leon, *Tools of the Mind: Vygotskian Approach to Early Childhood Education* (Upper Saddle River, NJ: Pearson, 2007), 74.

6 Seamus Heaney, "Scaffolding," *Poems, 1965-1975: Death of a Naturalist/Door Into the Dark/Wintering Out/North* (New York: Farrar & Strauss, 1966), 38.

7 UCLA Center for Mental Health in Schools, School Mental Health Project, "School Engagement, Disengagement, Learning Supports, & School Climate," (2011): 11, http://smhp.psych.ucla.edu/pdfdocs/schooleng.pdf.

8 Ibid., 9.

9 A few sources of learning materials: Learning Resources: http://www.learningresources.com/; EAI Education: http://www.eaieducation.com; Teacher Created Resources: http://www.teachercreated.com; Lakeshore Learning: http://www.lakeshorelearning.com/

10 Chip Wood, *Yardsticks: Children in the Classroom Ages 4-14* (Turners Falls, MA: NEFC, 2007), 64, 78, 100, 124.

11 Thomas Post, "Role of Manipulative Materials in the Learning of Mathematical Concepts," *Selected Issues in Mathematics Education*, National Society for the Study of Education and National Council of Teachers of Mathematics (Berkeley: McCutchan, 1981), 109.

12 Barbara Rogoff, *Apprenticeship in Thinking: Cognitive Development in Social Context* (New York: Oxford University Press, 1990), 193.

13 Gloria Ladson-Billlings, "Toward a Theory of Culturally Relevant Pedagogy," *American Educational Research Journal* 32, no. 3 (Autumn 1995): 473.

14 Sylvia Ashton-Warner, *Teacher* (New York: Simon & Schuster, 1963), 101.

15 Maxine Greene, "Diversity and Inclusion: Toward a Curriculum for Human Beings," *Teachers College Record* 95, no. 2 (Winter 1993): 218.

16 Linda Darling-Hammond, et al., *Powerful learning: What We Know about Teaching for Understanding* (San Francisco: Jossey-Bass, 2008), 4-5.

17 Arlette Ingram Willis, "Reading the World of School Literacy: Contextualizing the Experience of a Young African Male," *Harvard Educational Review* 65, no. 1 (Spring 1995): 32.

CHAPTER FOUR

Personalizing Whole Class Learning

The challenge in every classroom is to keep every student moving steadily toward proficiency in his or her learning. We have seen how personalized learning with the teacher, alone, or in small groups can meet this challenge. But some learning is best accomplished with everyone working together. To meet certain needs that every child has—the needs for relationship, community, competence, autonomy, and play—we have to create a culturally responsive environment in which each child:

- experiences a supportive, inclusive community that is largely self-managed, where his or her voice is heard
- learns by analyzing and constructing knowledge, as well as by listening and remembering, in ways that are personally meaningful and enjoyable
- develops academic skills like observation, listening, memory, analysis, and reflection, and social skills like self-awareness, self-regulation, self-expression, and leadership.

To accomplish such a tall order, students need each other. They need to assemble frequently for the kind of learning that comes from expressing and hearing diverse points of view. They need to listen to one another carefully, and learn ways of thinking and knowing that include their own logic and point of view along with those of others. They need to hear from everyone in the group so they understand each other better and learn to respect and appreciate the diversity of their class, their country, and their world.

Although some of the curriculum, such as incremental skill development, is often best taught one-to-one or in small groups, much learning at the elementary level occurs best through whole-class lessons. Such lessons can be personalized: they can take into account, in content and instruction, the cultures, interests, and strengths of all the students, and they can offer many opportunities for students to talk and to work with partners. Relationships are nurtured in whole-group discussions that involve everyone. Attunement grows and thrives among the children and between the teacher and the children as the group discusses, agrees and disagrees, plans, celebrates, and plays together, enjoying the conversations, the activities, and each other.

Including families

Families can be invited into whole-class learning experiences, as guests who will share with the class or to enjoy an activity with them. Their role is crucial, of course, for student performances, portfolio days, and conferences. Such occasions create and nurture trusting, effective partnerships between school and home.

Tailoring teaching to students

The orchestrator of this great work needs to know each of the children personally, culturally, and developmentally to make sure that everyone participates and has opportunities for leadership and self-expression. The better we know our students, the better we can teach them. We can connect their learning to their cultures, their developmental stages, and their interests and personalities.

"Culture, environment, health, temperament, and personality all affect the makeup of every child at every age. It's helpful that certain patterns have emerged and been documented, but they are never absolute."[1]

Learning Together in Community Circles

Use the whole-class circle for lessons that are just right and relevant for all students (as opposed to lessons for which some, but not all, are ready), and we can use the circle to spark learning and nurture relationships. The circle is a great equalizer in which everyone can see everyone, have a say, and be part of the whole. The circle invites us to be honest and to listen carefully to each other. We face each other with equality. The circle gives rise to insights from multiple points of view—360 degrees of understanding!

Power of the circle

Students can gather in the circle any time—not just at the start of the day—to connect with each other, learn together, plan a trip or celebration, or solve a problem. The circle is perfect for lively discussion and for critical thinking about complex issues. Its shape helps everyone think and behave democratically—it prepares children to become active citizens in our democracy. In the circle, students show appreciation for each other, celebrate accomplishments, and have fun.

The circle works especially well for whole-class lessons. Why sit looking at someone's back when you can sit face to face? The circle makes it much more likely that students will actively respond to *each other's* ideas, not just dialogue back and forth with the teacher. The objective is to increase student participation—thinking, talking, moving, leading—because the more active the learner, the better the learning.

I teach skip counting by walking around the circle in different ways for different types of counting while I tell the children a story with characters, such as the man with a cane. They become the character, thumping along: one, two, three, four.... (First grade teacher)

What follows are practices for academic and social learning enriched by community circles:

- Teaching effective mindsets for learning
- Starting the day, primed with a "morning challenge"
- Cultural conversations
- Power of play

- Closing the day
- Read-alouds and storytelling for reading, writing, and math
- Arts integration for reading, writing, and math
- Cognitive skill development
- Follow-ups
- Work-shares and performances

Community Circles for Healthy Learning Mindsets

Attitudes of mind have a huge effect on learning. A curious chid is a better listener and observer than an incurious one, and a child who believes that s/he will learn if s/he works hard is probably headed for success. A child who follows up an idea with action has the can-do spirit to accomplish a lot every day in school. Students' mindsets strongly influence efficacy in learning. We can influence their mindsets positively, improving their odds for success.

"Currently, theorists who have proposed models of achievement motivation posit that individuals' achievement-related beliefs, values, and goals are among the most important determinants of these outcomes."[2]

Curiosity mindset

Curiosity motivates students to engage in learning, and a good curriculum stimulates curiosity. For example, when a class gathers to read aloud or discuss a book, the teacher asks wondering questions: *Is there anything so far in this story that you wonder about? For example, I wonder why having a star on your belly was such a big deal for the Sneetches. Why do you think it was so important?*

I read a couple of pages from the book and stopped to ask if what we had read had them wondering about anything, and the hands went up. They started responding to each other's questions, and that was fun, too. It definitely got them thinking and engaged. It also helped them to see that the same picture or event could lead to many possibilities. What could it be? What could it mean? Imagine the possibilities. I told them that one of the great things about wondering is there are no wrong answers. They liked that. (First/second grade teacher)

Growth mindset

You can gather to read and do research about people who overcame disability. For example, in *If They Can Do It, We Can Too!*, students write about famous people who overcame learning differences similar to their own.[3] The Web has many resources that describe people who have overcome disability.[4] You can use a book like **Mistakes That Worked** to help children see possibilities in things that start out as mistakes.[5]

Yesterday I led a lesson about mistakes. I read to them stories about how mistakes can actually turn out to be wonderful things—fudge, Velcro, and so on. We discussed how if it hadn't been for mistakes, many inventions wouldn't have happened. I said, "Look at this piece of paper. I ripped a hole in the middle of it. I could think, 'Oh, no! It's ruined!' But what if I change my thinking? What could this hole in the middle of my paper become? Watch me turn it into something new and wonderful." I drew a picture around the hole so the hole became the center of a doughnut. The kids loved it. "Now it's your turn. Fold your paper and rip a hole in it. Look at the hole in a new way, and see what it can become. What can we turn our mistakes into?"

The funny part is that many of them were disappointed with their holes. One girl who accidentally tore her paper in half seemed stuck, so I reminded her that any mistake can turn into something brand new—you just have to look at it differently. She taped hers together into a crown and wore it happily!

We will remember this anchor lesson when we make mistakes in math or other parts of the day, especially socially, during recess. (First/second grade teacher)

A math lesson can include experiencing mistakes helping us learn. When children show each other how they solved a problem, they learn as they demonstrate their method or as they dialogue with classmates, or as they watch someone else reach the same answer by a different method.

We read the plan for the day and noted the problem that they would be sharing about at the end of the [math] lesson. We partnered up, and a couple of volunteers explained [how they reached] their answers. Everyone was interested and engaged.

They all checked their work, and when some realized their answer was different from what others were sharing, it sparked their interest. They seemed to focus more, to think about the problem and figure out where they went wrong. (First/second grade teacher)

Action mindset

An action mindset is the attitude of a problem-solver, a person who takes action when s/he is faced with a task or a question or a bump in the road. We can reinforce action-taking by rehearsing. Using hypothetical problems, we can pose academic or social dilemmas, and students can debate and decide on a course of action to resolve the dilemma. For example, imagine gathering together to discuss taking action in situations that might interfere with learning, such as:

- Someone keeps talking and joking and asking questions, and Maria can't concentrate and is getting annoyed. What can she do?
- Daniel is having a hard time doing his math and isn't sure he's getting it right. What can he do?
- David cuts into a line. Should other students say or do anything?

A Morning Challenge to Start the Day

When students enter the classroom, they can launch the day's learning with a challenge and connecting with a classmate. As they greet the teacher, they can receive an interesting task and a partner to do it with. The partners greet one another, using their names: "Hi, Mara;" "Hi, Victor," then start working on the challenge. They bring what they learn to the first community circle of the day to share with their classmates.

The morning challenge initiates learning for the day, sometimes in a directly academic way, sometimes not, but always in a way that builds social and cognitive skills:

- teaching and learning with a peer
- speaking and listening to each other independent of the teacher
- remembering, so they can share what they have done and learned

- regulating themselves to remain focused and responsive while working cooperatively
- planning to present their thinking to the whole group.

As you partner students, you can allow for any immediate student needs. Students who need to finish homework or eat breakfast might miss out on the challenge but aim for full participation. Consider scheduling enough time in the morning, before a morning circle or instruction begins, to allow for *both* miscellaneous student needs and the morning challenge.

During this early morning time you can catch up with students about whom you have concerns or who have recently had something important happen in their lives, or those you haven't chatted with for a while. Such informal exchanges help you keep up with their lives and allow you to gauge the mood of students so you can make sure to connect with those who might need support. If your conversation interrupts partners working on their morning challenge, one partner can work independently until the other returns.

The morning challenge, designed to satisfy the needs children have for interaction with peers and feelings of competence and independence, also cultivates three important cognitive skills: cognitive control, working memory, and language. All three help narrow the "... gulf between low and middle SES [socioeconomic status] children in their performance on just about every test of cognitive development."[6]

Examples of morning challenges

- Describe someone in your family (appearance, likes and dislikes, hobbies, employment, etc.)
- What would you do if... (someone said something that hurt your feelings; a person was told "You can't play with us!")
- Invent a hand-eye coordination game (supply materials: marbles, balls, hoops, sticks, etc.)
- Plan to lead a group game (a familiar one or one you invent)
- Create a challenging math problem and solve it
- Create a story plot (teacher might supply three characters and a setting)

- Teach us a word or phrase that some of us probably do not know (from a language other than English or from slang or a word you find in the dictionary)
- Figure the shortest path from Point A to Point B on a map (or in the classroom or from one place in the school to another, as directed by teacher)
- Invent a new word. Give its part of speech and definition
- Practice counting (by two's, three's, four's, or five's) as high as you can
- Illustrate the difference between two homophones

The partner activity first thing in the day generates enthusiasm for learning as the students arrive:

As for morning challenge, I love it and so do the kids. We've had so much fun! We've told jokes, and we drew a shape to decorate. Today students got to write a story together. I think they are more energized, engaged, and excited to get to school to find out what they are going to do with a partner. Today as students were arriving, one child was telling each of them, "We get to write stories today! We get to write stories today!" over and over. It is a great way to start the day! (Primary grades teacher)

First Circle of the Day

After ten or fifteen minutes (or longer, if appropriate) working on the morning challenge, give the signal to gather in the circle, or have a student do so. The first circle of the day connects everyone, includes some fun, and orients students to the day ahead.

First circle structure

1. **REPORT ON THE MORNING CHALLENGE:** Volunteers share about their morning challenge experience. Sometimes everyone gets a chance to share briefly. At the beginning of each person's sharing, he or she welcomes the class with "Good morning" or "Hola" or "Hi, everyone." The group responds, "Good morning, _____."
2. **ACTIVITY:** The group engages in an enjoyable activity—a game, a song, exercises, a dance, etc.
3. **LOOK BACK AND AHEAD:** the group reflects on the morning challenge or the activity or something from the previous day. The teacher outlines plans for the day, involving students in any decision making as much as possible.

Example start of the day in a first/second grade classroom

As students arrived, each was assigned a partner, and their task was to create a math problem for the class to solve. "Make sure you know the answer to your problem!" the teacher said. Most of the partnerships were made up of one first and one second grade student. Someone asked, "Can we do more than one?" and indeed every pair made up several problems. One second grader mused, "Maybe I should make up a problem my partner can do." Ten minutes later, the teacher gave the signal for everyone to gather for the first circle of the day.

Report on the morning challenge

"Sit next to your partner, and have your math problem ready to share." The teacher asked for volunteers to share a problem to solve. The pair she selected stood, and each greeted the class:
"Good morning, everyone."
"Good morning, Kevin."
"Good morning, everyone."
"Good morning, Beatrice." Kevin and Beatrice gave the

group one of the 'big' problems they had constructed: "What is 122 plus 122?"

The teacher directed: "Discuss this problem with your partner. When you agree on an answer, raise your hands." Soon hands shot up, and Beatrice called on Leon.

"244 is the answer!"

"How did you and Tiana get your answer?" Beatrice asked. Tiana explained: "We added one hundred and one hundred and got two hundred, then we added the twenties and got forty, then we added the two's and got four—two hundred, forty-four."

"Did anyone get the answer a different way?" Kevin asked.

He called on David, who said, "We added the two's, then the two's, then the ones, and got 244."

The group moved on to another problem. Other partners led, and students were eager to share how they got their answers. There was time for four pairs of partners to share their problems. Interest was high, and everyone would have liked to do more.

Activity

Next, the teacher introduced the math game Eleven. There was plenty of laughter while student groups attempted to hold up exactly eleven fingers at the same moment: Students form clusters of four, their hands behind their backs. On the leader's signal, group members instantly hold up fingers. Their goal each time is to show a total of eleven fingers. Collaborative strategizing is prohibited! Rule: students may not show the same number of fingers twice in a row.

Looking back and ahead

The group discussed how well it had worked when the partners worked on creating a problem. They said the second graders took turns with the first graders so each could invent problems. They shared how some second graders taught their first grade partners how to multiply. A first grader blurted out: "I finally know what that 'x' means!"

The teacher outlined what would happen that day and the next, and the meeting ended. The student who was the scheduler for the day signaled the next activity by moving the marker on the schedule, and the day was launched.

Community Circles for Cultural Conversations

Community circles are an excellent venue for students of various backgrounds to learn about and enjoy each other's lifestyles and points of view. When students talk with each other about their home cultures—the way they eat and play and the languages they use, how they celebrate, and what's important to them and their families—they grow. They learn about their classmates and come to feel known by them. They find out what they have in common. Stereotypes break down, and they increase their appetite for variety. Knowing and feeling known by their classmates and teacher lowers defensiveness and opens up possibilities for growth. A climate of mutual acceptance helps everyone thrive and succeed in school.

Community circle meetings designed intentionally for cultural conversations can help make acceptance happen. Following are two sample cultural conversations that demonstrate how circle meetings can lead to cultural understanding. They follow a simple pattern of engaging in a community-building rhythm, then an activity, and closing with a reflection. You may find a way to connect a cultural conversation to a book the class is reading or to a unit in social studies, or to a question you pose for a morning challenge to get students thinking about ways their cultures shape them.

Community-building rhythm

Begin the meeting with rhythm play, an activity that bonds and energizes a group. Students benefit socially (working as a team) and academically (building cognitive controls by focusing and remembering the patterns), building skills that are crucial for success in school, and they have fun. See Resources, page 181, for examples.

Cultural conversation about identity and diversity

This example describes a cultural conversation to help create a community in which everyone gets to know each other better.

Begin with a *community-building rhythm.*

ACTIVITY: THIS IS WHO I AM: Students may share with their classmates something about their lives outside of school. Each child gets an opportunity to share his/her family culture with the group in the following or other ways:

- Bring a member of the family to class
- Bring pictures of the family
- Share about food, activities, celebrations, music, dancing, language, jokes, events, travels, etc.
- Bring objects that represent an aspect of home (a recording, a significant object, a map to show where the family has been, etc.)
- Teach the class a word, song, dance, game, or joke that your family enjoys.

To support everyone's success in their This is Who I Am share, discuss the following questions with them. Post the list on the class Web site, and give everyone the questions to bring home and discuss with family.

- What country or countries did our family come from (recently or long ago)?
- How did you choose my name?
- What language(s) do people in our family know?
- What foods are part of our culture(s)?
- What jobs do people in our family have?
- Why do we celebrate the holidays we celebrate?
- Is anyone in our family disabled? Does anyone have a special talent or ability?
- How did we come to live where we do?

Further scaffolding can include:

- Brainstorming with children some questions you might ask one another to learn more
- Doing the first This is Who I Am share yourself and inviting children to ask questions. The first share serves as a rehearsal for students' cultural shares, and the above list is a mediator that supports the conversation when the sharer invites the class to respond to what he or she has shared.

REFLECTION: Partners discuss the following question: What did you learn about _____ (classmate) that you didn't know before? Invite partners to share with the group something they enjoyed learning from the This Is Who I Am share.

KEEP IN MIND: Some children may get more help from their families than others. To ensure that every This Is Who I Am share is meaningful, you may decide to contact the family yourself, or talk to a staff person who knows the family better than you do. To build clarity and confidence, preview with each student what he or she intends to share. You might want to invite family to attend their child's This is Who I Am share.

Cultural conversation about us vs. them

Begin with a *community-building rhythm* (see Resources, page 181, for examples).

ACTIVITY: COUNCIL: Using the Council process described below, lead students to discuss the question: Tell about a time when you or someone else was left out. How did you feel? Begin by stating the five rules, and check to make sure the children understand them:

- Everyone in the circle gets a chance to hold the talking stick and speak about the topic
- When one person is talking, everyone else is silent, listening carefully
- No one comments on what is said. There is no discussion of what anyone shares
- You may pass when the talking stick comes to you; after everyone else has had a turn, the stick can come back to you if you wish to speak
- What is said in Council stays in Council. Nobody repeats or discusses what they have heard in Council, including with others who were at the meeting.

You can model the process by speaking first. This is helpful when the Council process is new to the group, and any time the topic is challenging. When a student receives the stick, s/he tells about a time when s/he was excluded or s/he observed someone else being excluded, and s/he tells how s/he felt about it.

REFLECTION: Students record thoughts and images in journals or by using the How I Feel when I'm Left Out resource (see Resources, page 182) to stimulate deeper thinking and to store ideas for future writing.

Grades K-1: After the Council meeting, students draw the face of someone who has been left out (sad, lonely, angry, etc.).

Grades 2-5: After the Council meeting, students write and/or draw about what they said or about their feelings about the fact that we hurt others when we exclude them.

KEEP IN MIND: The talking stick is more meaningful if the group constructs and/or decorates it themselves. Use a fairly straight stick at least twelve inches long, and gather materials to decorate it: small objects from nature, ribbon, yarn, strips of fabric, etc., to add texture and color. Each student chooses something to add to the stick and does so. Anyone who joins the class later should add something to the talking stick before the next Council meeting.

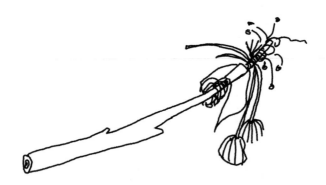

Community Circles for Read-alouds about Culture

An excellent way to build understanding across cultures is read-alouds of books that raise issues of prejudice and/or exclusion based on differences. Read-alouds create common ground for discussions of differences among cultures, issues of discrimination, and bullying. Talking about the dilemmas of story characters, making comparisons to our own lives, and seeking solutions help develop both the empathy to identify bigotry and the will to address it when it occurs. Following are a few of the many excellent books for such purposes. They are grouped by grade levels, but intermediate teachers have had excellent results using picture books to start honest conversations about cultural differences and exclusion.

Primary

Abuela by Arthur Dorros
Chrysanthemum by Kevin Henkes
Oliver Button is a Sissy by Tomie dePaola
The Sneetches and Other Stories by Dr. Seuss

Intermediate

Baseball Saved Us by Ken Mochizuki
In the Year of the Boar and Jackie Robinson by Bette Bao Lord
The Hundred Dresses by Eleanor Estes
Out of My Mind by Sharon M. Draper
Thank You, Dr. Martin Luther King, Jr. by Eleanora Tate

See also the University of Wisconsin bibliography on multicultural literature for children, *Multicultural Literature for Children and Young Adults.*[7]

Four-quarter diagram on exclusion

Many multicultural books deal with issues of exclusion. A follow-up to a discussion on a book about exclusion can be the following exercise, which encourages children to look at their own and others' behavior toward people who seem different from them.

Teach the word *exclude* and its antonym, *include*. Have children divide a paper into four quarters labeled:

- I was excluded....
- I excluded someone....
- I saw someone being excluded and said nothing....
- I saw someone being excluded and I spoke up....

Intermediate students write from their personal experiences on each of the four topics; primary students act out scenes for each of the four scenarios. After each scenario, ask students to raise their hands if they have experienced something like it themselves. Fill out the diagram yourself, share about your experiences, and invite volunteers to say more about theirs.

Community Circles for the Power of Play

Fun is important. It lifts spirits, focus, and energy when a class gathers for a moment of fun and laughter. Play is powerful because:

- the fun is inclusive—everyone joins in
- it's a moment of movement—an energy outlet for students for whom sitting still for a long time is particularly difficult
- when play is cooperative, everybody, whatever their skill level, gets to stay in the game
- play builds cognitive capacity for constructive thinking by creating problems to solve. It stimulates invention of variations, building skills and confidence
- play is universal. Cultures connect through the diversity and similarities in how they play.

There are hundreds of quick, playful activities, some that energize primarily through laughter, others that wake everyone up with physical movement. Visit The Origins Program Web site to find activities.[8] See four examples in Resources, page 183.

Imaginative play

In dramatic play, students re-enact life events using language, gesture, and movement (costumes and props are optional) to recreate an aspect of life they have experienced in fact or in stories. In dramatic play, they plan how characters will interact, what makes sense in the story and what doesn't. Negotiating all this with classmates requires thinking, articulating, listening, compromising, and remembering, among other cognitive skills. "Dramatic play permits children to fit the reality of the world into their own interests and knowledge. One of the purest forms of symbolic thought available to young children, dramatic play contributes strongly to the intellectual development of children."[9]

"In addition, extensive involvement in sociodramatic play seems to improve children's memory, language development, and cognitive perspective-taking abilities."[10]

For young children, imaginative drama with peers provides context for growth in the skills required to provide evidence for a point of view, to negotiate, to integrate thinking, to express oneself and listen to others' expressions, and generally to interact with others in a productive manner so we can enjoy ourselves and succeed in school at the same time.

"In such play, with pleasure, imagination, and involvement in devising and implementing rules, children free themselves from the situational constraints of everyday time and space and the ordinary meaning of objects or actions, to develop greater control of actions and rules and understanding. As such, play 'creates its own zone of proximal development of the child. In play a child is always above his average age, above his daily behavior; in play it is as though he were a head taller than himself.'"[11]

Play is a friend of learning. It can take students where we want them to go: to enthusiastic participation in their own growth.

Last Community Circle of the day

The community circle is the perfect format for rounding out the school day. It brings everyone together to share work, look back on what has been accomplished, and look ahead to plan for tomorrow, or to wish everyone well before weekends, holidays, and vacations. The last circle of the day is the time to acknowledge individuals for their contributions to the group, and to acknowledge accomplishments and kindnesses. See The Origins

Program Web site for acknowledgment activities such as Touch Someone Who and Pretzel.[12]

Community Circles for Reading, Writing, and Math

Lessons that incrementally move children toward mastery of skills in reading, writing, or math are usually best taught through personalized learning in small groups or one-to-one. Many other kinds of lessons are perfect for the community circle format. In order for such lessons to also be personalized, they need to be relevant to a variety of learners, and they need to invite listening, thinking, and exchange of experiences and ideas among everyone. Everyone can participate because everyone can bring life experiences to the discussion. Some lessons are informational—a science demonstration, for example; others are opportunities to analyze, wonder, ask questions, and draw conclusions about events in history or in a story. Whole-class lessons must be relevant and appropriate for everyone.

Read-alouds and storytelling

Read-alouds can help children learn to love literature and to understand its components. Absorbing a book together, children can talk about plot, setting, and characters, and about issues raised in the story that are relevant to their own lives. Shared books about people and problems that interest everyone stimulate thinking and talking about our own lives.

Fiction about people from various cultures

The Hundred Dresses[13] provides context for talking about bullying and loyalty to friends. In Knots on a Counting Rope,[14] the bravery of a boy with a handicap in a tribal community stimulates sharing about moments of fear and courage, and the power of elders in our lives.

As stories are shared, partners can talk with each other about challenging social situations. They can ask each other why Maddie went along with teasing Wanda, and how the blind boy found the courage to race on a horse. Allow enough time for both partners to talk about what they would do in the situation the book presents. See Learning to be a Partner, page 135, for preparing children to partner productively.

After their partner work, everyone returns to the circle for a whole-group discussion of the story: the relationships, behaviors, motivations, cause and effect, points of view, prediction, analysis, evidence-gathering, and so on. These skills and understandings will be used again and again in their educational careers.

Nonfiction books from and about various cultures

Read-alouds of nonfiction, too, can spark lively whole-class discussions and follow-up activities. In the circle, children talk with partners about what they have heard. The book may be the basis of a follow-up project by partners, or students may work individually on topics stimulated by the book, then gather to show and explain their work to each other.

Both imaginative stories and accounts of real events can be shared in the classroom through storytelling. Young people enjoy telling stories, and many learn to write by starting with their own stories.

A class of about 25 third and fourth graders were engaged in making pâpier-maché masks. A visiting artist sat at one of the tables, helping. In a quiet voice he began, "Once when I was a boy...." Everyone stopped what they were doing and looked at him and listened! The magic words that were clearly the beginning of a story captured them immediately. (Educational consultant)

Community Circles for Art Integration

Drama

Dramatization brings learning alive in the classroom because most elementary-age students are visual and kinesthetic learners. Seeing and moving are doorways to learning for almost everyone, and for some learners they are essential to focusing and remembering. Reenactments and storytelling about moments or periods in history, or imagined conversations between historical figures, make the past vivid and memorable. Important reading skills such as the ability to visualize what you are reading are boosted by dramatic representations of texts.

One teacher taught her second graders for a day in the style of European-American colonial schools with desks in rows and students standing at attention to recite facts. A fifth grade teacher had students set up "shops" in the medieval manner, and when it was time for social studies, the baker and butcher and blacksmith and others all went to their shops, while other students—townspeople—shopped and chatted before going on with their day. A fourth grade teacher invited a few friends to enact a town council meeting, and students petitioned the council to vote against construction proposed for a nearby area where they liked to play. The students who had these experiences are not likely to forget them, or the facts and concepts they learned.

We acted out a book today, and we had so much fun! I picked a picture book that we had read previously so students were familiar with the story. I read it and picked students to be certain characters as we went along. Students were standing and sitting and moving about, all engaged and having fun. [The principal] peeked in to see what all the commotion was about. It was a reading lesson, and we talked about how readers imagine or try to picture what they are reading....We will definitely be doing this again. (Primary grades teacher)

Theater can also be used to build language and math skills. A memorable way to teach reading vocabulary is to have students act out the meaning of a word while others guess the word from the ones on their lists. In math, word problems can be posed in the form of a simple narrative (which children might even act out).

Minnie Minus has ten acorns, and she gives three to her babies. How many acorns does Minnie have left? Show us with your fingers. Timmy Times has three groups of acorns and each group has three acorns in it. How many acorns in all does Timmy have? (Children draw the acorns as the story is told.) *Show us with your fingers.* (First grade teacher)

Social skills can be addressed and practiced through role plays: what do you do and say in a difficult situation to speak up for yourself, be fair, be a friend to others, and meet your own needs? Children can act out the scene and try various approaches.

Movement

Other art forms also make memorable impressions. A math teacher introduced her students to tessellations through movement that became synchronized dances; a fourth grade teacher taught her students about the geography of river beds through original dances that students performed for each other. A kindergarten teacher coaches students in self-regulation as she beats a rhythm on a drum: they stop, start, skip, hop around the room, avoiding bumping each other, listening carefully so they freeze when the drum stops. Invite students to move as they learn, and you will see fresh interest and engagement, especially among students who have a hard time sitting still for long periods of time. Learning while they move is learning *their* way.

Music

A fifth grade class loved to sing together and did so most days. They decided to create an album singing their favorite songs. This required getting permission to use copyrighted music in their recording. They wrote letters and made phone calls, and got the permissions. They made the recording in a studio, wrote an explanatory piece, and created a handsome cover for the CD, and everyone in the class took home a copy at the end of the year.

A primary teacher uses songs to signal that it's time for a transition. At a signal from her, the students quietly transition to their work stations or circle up or put away their materials or line up.

Visual arts

After a lesson on the proportions of the human face, first and second grade teachers had students declare their goals for the year by creating self-portraits and attaching to them declarations of what they wanted to learn. Kindergartners in that school created family trees that included friends and pets as well as relatives. In another school, first- and second-graders drew portraits of characters in books they had read, accompanied by written comments about them. They began with an oval for the face, surrounded by clouds in which they wrote. They included traits the student had in common with the characters and their wonderings about the characters. See a student example opposite.

After a walking field trip, another primary group created a model of the neighborhood around their school, using cardboard, construction paper, and lots of glue.

Poetry

Among its other virtues, poetry writing often elicits authenticity and surprising depth. It helps learners become comfortable with language and use it *their* way to say what they think and feel. A third grader wrote this poem about exclusion:

"You can't play," they said.
It looked like they were having fun
And I really wanted to be a part of it.
I really wanted to join them.
"You can't play," they said.
They didn't think I was good enough to be on their team.
They were afraid I would make them lose.
"But I'm better at it than they are," I thought.
"You can't play," they said.
"Well, I don't want to anyway," I said.
But I really did.

A fourth grader wrote this poem about the ways everyone is connected to everyone, no matter how much they differ:

We're all different—we're all the same.
We all have different amounts of money and things—but we all need love, care, and attention.
Some of us are boys and some of us are girls—but everyone alive has a heart.
People are born with different color skin, like black, brown, and peach—but everyone needs clothes in COLD states like Minnesota.
Some people are better than others at things like sports—but we all need food to live.
People talk differently—but we all need water.
We all look different from each other—but we all get mad, laugh, and cry.
We're all different—we're all the same.

Welcoming uniqueness

Theater, movement, music, visual art, and poetry help us look
from different points of view and deal with the world flexibly, ex-
perimentally, and with questions. (For ideas on integrating arts
into your practice, see *Lively Learning: Using the Arts to Teach the
K-8 Curriculum* by Linda Crawford.[15]) "Providing a decent place
for the arts in our schools may be one of the most important
first steps we can take to bring about genuine school reform."[16]

The arts invite children to be and express themselves authentically. When we welcome children's creative expressions,
we welcome their individuality and we personalize learning. We
show that we value them as they really are, which is the affirma-
tion they need to be and do their very best.

Community Circles for Cognitive Skill Development

Some of the best learning in whole-class instruction happens during the development of cognitive skills that can be applied in any learning context, such as observation, deliberate memory, and perspective-taking.

Observation

There are many ways children can sharpen their capacity to notice carefully and accurately:

- A partner game where one person carefully describes an object inside a box and the other guesses from the description what it is
- A circle game where partners mime using a common object for surprising purposes, and children guess what they are pretending the object is
- Class observation of a painting or photograph, pointing out as many details as they can
- Partners draw each other, showing as much detail as they can (they take turns drawing and sitting for their partners)
- Observational drawing of an object where the goal is to reproduce what you see as accurately as possible

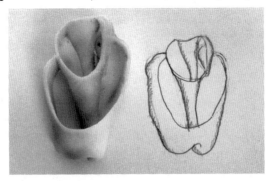

I told students that one activity that helps people to learn is noticing. If you don't notice something, it's almost like it's not there, or it didn't happen. The first step to learning something is noticing (I also use the term "paying attention"). I reminded them that they've already had some practice with this when they give "I noticed" closing comments. I told them that today they were going to give "I notice" statements about a piece of art. I stressed that art is different for every person

who views it: "I get to say what I see and you get to say what you see. Nothing else." They understood. The noticing was a huge success! They were engaged, coming up to the picture and pointing. At the end we read a little bit about it and found something that nobody had noticed (a sword). I think that experience will inspire them to be even more observant next time. (First/second grade teacher)

These children later used their observational powers in a science lesson on rocks. They each got a rock to observe, then drew it as accurately as possible. Later, all the rocks were mixed together, and the challenge the group had was to match each drawing with its rock.

We gathered in the circle with the drawings and rocks in the center. They looked very carefully, and when someone thought they saw a match, they identified it for us. The first rocks to be paired with their pictures were ones with a distinctive mark, like a red line or a yellow circle. Others were harder, but mostly they had observed and drawn so carefully that they were able to correctly match up the rocks and pictures. At the end, there were only a few rocks and pictures we weren't sure of. (First/second grade teacher)

Other options for the application of observational skills include writing down what you notice about the descriptive details of a character in a story; noticing plants and animals in science lessons and drawing them accurately; noticing objects in a museum or on a walk carefully enough to get past the obvious and observe details. Careful observation is fun, and students enjoy getting good at what their teacher knows is an important cognitive skill.

Deliberate memory

Noticing can be followed by deliberately remembering and then recalling what you saw. After observing a group of objects, the children can try to name all of them after they have been removed from sight. Or they can observe a scene or object carefully, then draw it from memory. In these early years, human memory has great capacity, so this is a time to cultivate memorization: poems, songs, verses, names of places and parts of things. Students can recite daily something they have memorized.

We have children memorize verses that they recite, poems, the words to songs, parts in plays, melodies for their recorders, in addition to memorizing math and other facts and retelling stories. Purposeful memorizing helps develop their will. In general, they seem to focus better because they must focus to remember. And when they know something by heart, they have more feeling for it; it goes deeper. We make sure to balance all that memorizing with lots of opportunities for creativity and self-expression. (First through eighth grade teacher)

Lots of circle games cultivate memory. Going on a Picnic, Alibi, Around the World, Category Snap, and other cumulative remembering games, for example, build good listening skills as well as memory. Visit www.OriginsOnline.org for hundreds of classroom games, many of which build memory.

Reflection

Another important cognitive skill that can be built during community circles is reflection. Children need to be able to look back on their work and their experiences and comment on what was helpful, what they enjoyed, what was difficult, and what was especially successful. All competent adults reflect to grow in skill and understanding. The learning community can reflect together during the day—after lessons, study sessions, work on projects, reading and writing workshops, field trips, and performances. They can ask themselves dozens of important questions, and the answers can guide their continued learning.

"Reflection is a basic human ability (a) to consider the goals, motives, methods, and means of one's own and other people's actions and thoughts...(b) to take other people's points of view; view things from perspectives other than one's own; and (c) to understand oneself; study one's own strong points and limitations in order to find the ways to excel or to accept one's shortcomings. Introspection is one part of this remarkable human faculty; the power for self-changing and transcending one's limitations is another component of the human ability for reflection."[17]

Community Circles to Launch Follow-ups

Community circles can be springboards for working on projects. Group demonstrations, explanations, and conversations stimulate ideas for where a learner might go next, especially when the teacher invites students to explore further.

- A discussion about slavery as it existed for generations in the American South sparked sixth graders' interest in researching and tracing the Underground Railroad and retelling the stories of the people who helped escapees run for their lives.

- Reading aloud a book about immigrant children sparked interest in reading first-person fictional narratives about immigrant children. Students evoked the characters they had read about as their teacher interviewed them in a simulation activity.

- Learning about the rotation of the earth around the sun inspired two fifth grade boys to construct a sun-at-noon monitoring station. The boys covered a section of window with a paper containing a small hole. Every day for a month, the boys carefully marked where the sun came through the hole and fell on a paper mounted on the opposite wall, noting the exact place the light struck the paper at noon each day, thus capturing its rising arc to March 21, the spring equinox.

All of these projects fit into the curriculum. They required children to exercise the skills they were honing in reading, writing, science, and math. To use educator Eleanor Duckworth's delightful phrase, they invited "the having of wonderful ideas."[18]

Community Circles for Work Shares and Performances

Frequent opportunities to see each other's work boost the incentive to produce good work, and work shares and performances are opportunities for students to lead and to be heard among their peers. When a child is presenting, he or she is the leader, and has a chance to experience positive, affirming group interest and approval. It also equalizes certain dynamics in the classroom, where poor children are often on one side of a wide cultural and power gap between them and the teacher. "The teacher cannot be the only expert in the classroom. To deny students their own expert knowledge *is* to disempower them."[19]

Frequent sharing changes the experience of work. It becomes something students do in anticipation of a response from their peers, not just from the teacher. Regularly inviting students to share their work with the class shows respect for their work and value for the diverse voices in the class, with no one left out.

Scaffold for quality whole-class work shares

Make the most of audience exchanges by laying the groundwork for quality inquiry. Brainstorm questions to ask about someone's work:

- Is this finished, or would you like to work on this some more?
- What is your favorite part? Why?
- Is there anything you are dissatisfied with? Why?
- As you were working on this, where did you make changes? Why did you make those changes?
- Did you enjoy doing this work? What was the most (or least) enjoyable part?
- If you were going to do this again, how would you make it better?

Scaffold students' audience skills through rehearsal and partner practice. When they are ready to be active listeners and supportive inquirers, let the work shares begin!

REHEARSAL: To coach for a quality experience of their first performance, have students rehearse the roles of presenter and audience. Begin with a work sample from a previous year; the teacher takes the role of the work presenter and answers questions students ask (they may use their brainstormed list).

PARTNERS: Pairs share and ask about each other's work for about ten minutes, using questions from the list.

WHOLE CLASS: A student shares a piece of work with the whole group and answers questions from the audience, who use the brainstormed list as well as new questions.

The usefulness of an audience—especially an audience of one's peers—can hardly be overstated. Assuming the classroom culture is safe and inclusive, the diversity of questions makes for varied and interesting responses. Whenever a student presents work or performs in front of others, s/he is called toward excellence, if for no other reason than the desire to be admired.

Opportunities for performance, great and small, occur frequently in an ordinary school day. There are the major events to which families as well as others in the school may be invited, but on any day we can whet children's appetite for excellence by providing a bit of time for them to share with one another some work that they have done. A community circle after a work period can include one or two people showing or talking about their work. If there is time, others can comment or ask questions:

- Did you make the gameboard yourself?
- How do you keep score?
- What does your diorama look like so far?

A Climate that Empowers Learning in Community

Effective community circles require healthy relationships and knowing how to learn together. These connections and skills can be created and nurtured in the circle, and the circle becomes an apprenticeship in social learning, in intentionally listening to each other. Careful listening helps everyone stay connected and feel valued. Engagement happens when children have a say and when they grow in self-regulation and responsibility.

The considerations and practices that follow nurture an inclusive culture enlivened by productive partnerships, increasing student leadership and autonomy, and enjoyment of one another as they work and play together.

Seating

Change up seating arrangements now and then, so that eventually, everyone sits near and partners with everyone else. *What are some fun ways we can mix up seating each day so we all get to know one another? Shall we make a game of it?*

- *Find someone whose name begins with the same letter as yours and sit next to each other in the circle.*
- *If you are a boy, sit next to a girl, and vice versa.*
- *Sit next to someone you haven't spoken to today.*

Each day we'll have a challenge to mix us up so we all become friends and work partners.

Participation

In effective community circles, the focus of learning is on each other, on ideas exchanged, problems solved, and having fun learning together. The circle encourages students to respond to each other, not just to the teacher. The challenge for the teacher is to consciously limit his or her own talking, and use group protocols to prompt active discussions with broad participation. The teacher must teach and mediate group participation protocols, and students must rehearse the expectations for group participation, then join in group activities and discussions.

Managing conversations so everyone is heard

Beyond the usual practice of the teacher calling on students who raise their hands, there are many other ways for deciding who will speak, and how often. We can use a variety of techniques to get everyone in the circle involved and thinking, to generate as much participation as possible by everyone, with no silent outsiders. For example, after a student responds to a question, s/he can call on another student, who, after speaking, calls on someone else. A lively, inclusive conversation ensues with little or no direction from the teacher. Voilà: student autonomy in a safe, orderly context! See The Origins Program Web site for other ways to manage group conversations so everyone is heard.

Centers and other group learning routines

Here is how one teacher employs centers for use of science kits:

We did Explosion Blowout Science, woven into our literacy time. We were able to meet with all seven reading groups and provide the tier-two intervention groups their time. Using the informational text from the science kit as well as other resources, we had meaningful [small-group] discussions at all levels of learning. I used alpha boxes for some of the groups. Other groups had the text cards from the kit and played "Find the Rock and Support your Idea with Evidence."

We processed with the students afterward. They loved doing science in small groups, explaining that it was easier to share and to listen to others. They asked for a center stocked with books from which they could choose for their reading and research. They also asked for a word game center. Talk about a rich afternoon! Although it took high energy and five center changes during that time, we found that the quality of learning was increased substantially. (Third grade teacher)

In addition to centers, there are many other formats to structure group learning. The goal is to provide opportunities for significant peer-to-peer work.

QUOTE JIGSAW PEER-TO-PEER FORMAT: Students are divided into groups of four. Each group selects or is given text—a quote, or a paragraph or page in a book—which they read aloud, then discuss what it means and why it is interesting and/or important. All the groups can use the same text, or each group can have a different one. When the groups have concluded their discussions, the students in each small group count off one through four, and all the 1's, the 2's, the 3's, and the 4's form new groups of four. In the new groups, students again discuss the meaning of the text and why it is interesting and/or important. In this activity, students practice forming opinions and articulating them and listening to others' thinking.[20]

Learning to be a partner

Beyond the quick exchanges of Turn and Talk in which partners talk about a topic for a minute or two, other peer-to-peer structures provide enough time for partners to think through a question or talk about a book and come up with more complex, collaborative answers, insights, and comments. As every teacher knows, allowing students to talk with each other can lead to off-task chat. Peer-to-peer interactions succeed when they have been rehearsed ahead of time and are supported with mediators such as prompts, visuals, or timers.

Rehearsing

In the first few weeks of school, introduce, discuss, and rehearse the roles and responsibilities of being a partner. Have discussions and rehearsals after long vacations, before an event such as a field trip, or periodically, just to avoid slipping. Use rehearsals to explore concepts such as the differences between partners and friends, and shared responsibility for outcomes.

Forming partnerships

To build an inclusive community that is friendly to everyone, vary the means by which partners are established. You can use random methods like pulling name sticks or using categories like a person whose name starts with the same letter as yours, or, to ensure that everyone gets a turn partnering with everyone else, you can set up a partner rotation system.

Opportunities for partnering

You can set up different sets of buddies for different purposes: classroom job partners, reading partners, writing partners, line partners for walking in the halls, academic game partners (three or four students who rotate roles such as player and fact-checker), playground partners, and more.

You and the children can identify times when partners would be helpful (consider cross-classroom and before- and after-school activities partnerships). Frequent and varied opportunities for children to talk, listen, and work with partners build their speaking and listening skills and increase their opportunities to think and learn through interaction with others. "The collaborative process seems to lead to a level of understanding unavailable in solitary endeavor or noncollaborative interaction."[21]

Collaboration seems particularly crucial to help children develop creativity and abilities to solve problems. Peer-to-peer interaction allows for student autonomy and leverages the competency of the partners. See Chapter Three, page 90, for more about effective partnerships.

Scaffolding student leadership

Leading small groups of their peers nurtures social and academic skills in students. They learn to organize, to remember a procedure and the content that is the focus of the gathering, to articulate accurately, to remain focused even when there are distractions, to assert themselves, and more. Group leaders manage their own behavior in order to command respect and keep the group focused. The incentive is great, because the support of peers is highly valued. Leadership opportunities support individual growth for all learners. They require that the teacher introduce the process and expectations for leadership, that s/he conduct rehearsal(s), and that s/he offer any mediators that will help student leaders remember what to do and how and when to do it. See Chapter Five, page 148, for examples of student leadership and how to establish these skills.

Educating Everyone

Through individual, partner, and whole-group learning, we encourage student-to-student interaction and every student's voice to be heard, because these are practices that make school relevant and meaningful for all children. Frequent opportunities for student self-expression, creativity, knowledge construction, and leadership satisfy young people's needs for good relationships and a sense of their own competency and autonomy. When all of this occurs in a school where students and their families are respected, appreciated, and informed, and where learning is personalized so each child progresses from success to success, we can educate equitably, with no one left behind.

Reflections

What do you currently use whole-class gatherings for?

What other uses of the community circle are you interested in trying in your classroom?

How might you begin having cultural conversations with students?

What ideas do you have for adding more movement, arts, and play or fun to your classroom day?

How do you utilize partners in your classroom? What ideas from this chapter might you want to add?

What have you learned about scaffolding in this chapter that might influence your teaching?

1   Chip Wood, *Yardsticks: Children in the Classroom Ages 4-14* (Turners Falls, MA: NEFC, 2007), xv.

2   Alan Wigfield and Jacquelynne S. Eccles *Development of Achievement Motivation* (San Diego: Academic Press, 2002), 1.

3   Margo Holden Dineen, *If They Can Do It, We Can Too! Kids Write About Famous People Who Overcame Learning Differences Similar to Theirs* (Minneapolis: Fairview Press, 1992).

4   Renee Jacques, "16 Wildly Successful People Who Overcame Huge Obstacles To Get There," *Huffpost Healthy Living*, The Huffington Post, http://www.huffingtonpost.com/2013/09/25/successful-people-obstacles_n_3964459.html.

5   Charlotte Jones, *Mistakes That Worked: 40 Familiar Inventions and How They Came to Be* (New York: Random House, Delacourt Press, 1991).

6   Martha Farah, Kimberly Noble, and Hallam Hurt, "Poverty, Privilege, and Brain Development: Empirical Findings and Ethical Implications," *Neuroethics: Defining the Issues in Theory, Practice, and Policy*, ed. J. Illes (Oxford: Oxford University Press, 2004), 278.

7   Cooperative Children's Book Center, School of Education, University of Wisconsin-Madison, "Multicultural Literature," http://ccbc.education.wisc.edu/books/multicultural.asp.

8   See www.OriginsOnline.org/games#for-elementary.

9   Jean Piaget, *Comments on Vygotsky's critical remarks concerning The Language and Thought of the Child, and Judgment and Reasoning in the Child*, trans. and ed. E. Hanfmann and G. Vakar (Cambridge: The MIT Press, 1962).

10 Fergus P. Hughes, "Spontaneous Play in the 21st Century," *Contemporary Perspectives on Play in Early Childhood Education*, ed. Olivia N. Saracho and Bernard Spodek (Greenwich, CT: Information Age Publishing, 2003), p.23.

11 L.S. Vygotsky, *Mind in Society: The Development of Higher Psychological Processes* (Cambridge: Harvard University Press, 1978), 102.

12 See www.OriginsOnline.org/acknowledgments-cheers-closings#all.

13 Eleanor Estes, *The Hundred Dresses* (New York: Harcourt, 1944).

14 Bill Martin Jr. and John Archambault, *Knots on a Counting Rope* (New York: Henry Holt, 1987).

15 Linda Crawford, *Lively Learning: Using the Arts to Teach the K-8 Curriculum* (Turners Falls, MA: Northeast Foundation for Children, 2004).

16 Elliot W. Eisner, "Misunderstood Role of the Arts in Human Development," *Phi Delta Kappan*, April 1992, 591.

17 Galina Zuckerman, "Development of Reflection through Learning Activity," *European Journal of Psychology of Education* 2004, Vol XIX 9-18.

18 Eleanor Duckworth, *The Having of Wonderful Ideas and Other Essays on Teaching and Learning* (New York: Teachers College Press, 2006.

19 Lisa Delpit, *Other People's Children: Cultural Conflict in the Classroom* (New York: New Press, 1995/rev. 2006), 32-33.

20 Quote Jigsaw is adapted from *Student Groups that Work: Everyday Learning Routines for Meaningful Interaction, Grades 5-9* (Minneapolis: The Origins Program, publication pending). Many structures in this book for grades 5-8 are also suitable for intermediate grades.

21 Barbara Rogoff, *Apprenticeship in Thinking: Cognitive Development in Social Context* (New York: Oxford University Press, 1990), 178.

CHAPTER FIVE

Managing the Learning Day

When we gather to learn in classes of 20 to 30 students, we seek ways to manage the day to ensure that each child in the group gives maximum attention to learning. This means that the lessons must engage the learners—meet them at their skill and interest levels. It means that students must learn in ways that are most effective for them—sometimes within the whole class, sometimes in small groups or with partners, and sometimes one to one with a teacher. It means that transitions throughout the day must be quick and designed and led at various times by everyone in the room so that everyone is invested in the smooth running of the day. And it means that disruptions need to be handled in a way that minimizes their negative effects on everyone. We manage the day right along with teaching the academic curriculum. Carefully designed routines help us succeed in both.

Sharing Responsibility

We need to explain this to children: *We use routines to get less important things done quickly and well so we have as much time as possible for more important things. Our routines need not be bothersome or time-consuming. We want to grow in reading and writing and math; we want to grow in leadership and cooperation; and we want time for fun, invention, and thoughtful questions. Good routines, smoothly carried out, help us get what we want.*

Collaboratively made and executed routines allow teachers and students to construct "democratic, reciprocal, and inclusive school climates."[1] We enjoy school and learn more when we work together as a community to 1) share responsibility to make the day go well; 2) anticipate the breakdowns that surely will occur; and 3) reflect: everyone thinks about how things are going and what could be improved. Routines that allow as much student self-management and independence as possible deepen students' satisfaction and engagement in learning at the same time. Routines allow everyone to share responsibility for the well-being of the class.

Satisfying the needs for competence and autonomy

Creating routines together reduces the feeling of being bossed around. If you are used to spontaneity, moving when you feel like it, and saying what you want when you want, shifting to a classroom community takes a lot of adjustment. Helping shape the day and assisting in guiding each other through it allows a sense of autonomy in a situation that, at first, can feel not only unfamiliar, or even foreign, to a child, but also arbitrary and unfair.

The list of needed routines is long: entering the classroom, taking attendance, the lunch count, classroom jobs, the signal(s) for attention, handing in homework, passing out papers and materials, asking questions, getting materials, going to the nurse, and on and on. Many schools spend a significant amount of time during the first few weeks of school establishing and rehearsing routines, because good routines mastered early in the year by everybody make for a more positive learning environment. Children can participate in figuring out how to facilitate a schedule that works for everyone.

What is the best way for us to handle the daily snack? How can we take care of our classroom supplies so they are not wasted or messy? How loud should our voices be so we can talk to each other and others can still concentrate?

If I am part of the problem, I want to be part of the solution.

Schedules and Transitions

Things often go wrong during transitions, putting this group of routines among the most important for many teachers. Moving from desks or tables to the circle, or moving chairs, or forming small groups to work with or without the teacher, or pairing up for work, or spreading out for silent reading, or lining up to go to the gym or the lunchroom or recess, or a handful of students gathering for a pull-out session—all of these transitions can be done quietly and efficiently. At the same time, students can build the self-regulation skills necessary for successful learning.

Self-regulation in transitions

Transitions fueled by self-regulation help everyone remain engaged, focused, and calm. Collaboration with students to manage routines pays off in less disruption during transitions. *How will we know it's time to stop doing one thing and start another? How shall we manage the rhythm of our day? Let's plan how we will move from one place to another or change from one activity to another as we follow our schedule.*

Self-regulation is a crucial skill. With it, children are ready and able to learn; without it, they are unfocused and a potential distraction to others. Self-regulation keeps learners on task, even if they begin to tire; it inspires learners to persevere through discouragement and setbacks. It pulls them past initial lack of interest in a topic or activity, into the realm of possibility. Socially, self-regulation restrains students from interrupting or speaking off the topic of discussion. It makes it possible for energized children to sit still, and for all to engage in games, large-motor activity, and recess fun without losing control.

"Self-regulation is a critical competency that underlies the mindful, intentional, and thoughtful behaviors of younger and older children alike. The term self-regulation (sometimes also called executive function) refers to the capacity to control one's impulses, both to stop doing something, if needed (even if one wants to continue doing it) and to start doing something, if needed (even if one doesn't want to do it). Self-regulation is not to be confused with obedience or compliance; when children are truly self-regulated they behave the same way whether or not an adult is watching."[2]

Self-regulation can be learned in very pleasant ways. For example, coaching children to start and stop in response to a rhythmic movement to music takes body as well as mind control, both of which are needed in the classroom. Rhythms without movement (for example, in limited space) can teach the same thing in another way:

I came up with a way to use drumming at the beginning of my small groups every day during our leveled reading rotations…I start out by [drumming with my hands] on the table or on my shoulders. I look around and continue my drumming pattern until all students have caught on and are following me. Then, without talking, [I] change my pattern—I do this several times. After my turn, I point to a student to take over as leader, and he or she leads three or four different sequences. Three students take the lead each day. They have embraced this activity and now volunteer and take the lead at the beginning of each small group. I love this activity because it brings us together, builds community within our small group, helps us focus, and allows students to have control right away before getting into the content of the lesson. [When they drum], students are continually practicing self-control and are able to show us their creative side, which I love. I noticed two outcomes so far:…students are more engaged during small group, and…there are fewer behavioral challenges. (English for Specific Purposes teacher K-3)

Self-regulating with mediators

Mediators—usually visual and auditory reminders about what to do and when to do it—help make orchestrating the day a collaboration between teacher and children. These supports replace some or all of the teacher direction otherwise needed for managing routines.

Display the schedule

When does the school day start and stop? When is lunch? Recess? When do we have music? Create and post the schedule so everyone can see the framework for the day. Include a movable indicator to point to the current activity. With young children, use pictures. Let one of the classroom jobs be "schedule watcher," the person who moves the indicator when it's time to move to the next activity. Like all classroom jobs, serving as schedule watcher fulfills the needs for competence and autonomy. See Resources, page 175, for a sample schedule.

Signs, timers, and partners

Using mediators like signs and timers, students can follow as well as lead procedures the class has rehearsed. To begin a transition, a student leader can circulate silently, holding up a sign that says "Clean up now" or "Join the circle" or "Line up now." The sign gives the instruction, and the silence increases efficiency and encourages student autonomy. Partners can support one another in transitions. If one sees the sign or other mediator, he or she can point it out to the other. A timer and a recording chart can challenge the group to try to beat the clock or achieve their best time yet.

Music

Some classes sing their way through transitions, thus reducing stress. The group can agree that a particular song will indicate a certain transition. Thereafter, when the children hear "Twinkle, Twinkle," for example, they head for the circle, and "You Are My Sunshine" means it's time to line up. This practice replaces spoken direction with the pleasure of singing while you move. To increase children's investment in orderly transitions, starting the song can be a classroom job: *Alissa, please signal our transition to circle.* Alissa begins singing or turns on the recording, enjoying her feeling of competence. Or the leader of the transition, a student or the teacher, can start a rhythm, and others can pick it up. Because classroom jobs rotate periodically, the children know they are collaborators in the larger plan for them to share responsibility and leadership, and each will get a turn.

Here are some comments from primary level teachers who have established self-regulated transitions using music:

Yesterday we came up with a list of songs to sing at that time. We talked about length—that we couldn't pick a short song if we need time to clean up, and we couldn't pick a song with actions! They loved being part of the process. Today I set the timer and said if they see that time is almost up, they could start the song. This was a hilarious disaster. When the timer got below five minutes, there were at least ten kids standing around it waiting for it to run out! I guess I need to pick a student each day who gets to start the song.

Today I introduced singing during cleanup. I started by introducing a call-and-response song that we had sung earlier in the year. As I started the lesson I said, "I have noticed that cleanup can take a long time. We want to talk and share about our work while we are cleaning, and it slows us down. There is a saying, 'whistle while you work.' People like to sing or whistle to keep their minds focused on what they are doing. It makes work more fun!" I introduced the song with a CD, and we generated new lyrics to make the song about cleanup. This was really fun, and there was a lot of buy-in. I told them we would try it out today with me being the leader, and when we get really good at the song, the students could lead the cleanup song themselves. Their faces lit up when they heard that!

Today, I used the cleanup song to transition from readers' workshop, and we cleaned up so quickly we were four minutes early for lunch! I celebrated with the kids by acknowledging the positive points of cleanup—quick, thorough, fun, and exciting. I said, "What should we do with our extra time? Let's play a game!" We then played Number Squeeze to pass the time.

Student leadership

Leading transitions empowers children. Of course, leadership for transitions must be taught and rehearsed. Consider the process for establishing a student line leader: *When you are the line leader, you have to have everyone line up in an orderly way, remind everyone of how to walk in the halls, and lead the line to our destination.* The teacher demonstrates the procedure, pointing out important details, then the teacher or a volunteer leads a rehearsal. Before a child leads the lineup routine, a verbal review with that child will set him or her up for success.

Student-led dismissal

After teaching and rehearsing, the teacher may include dismissing classmates from the circle on the list of classroom jobs. To ensure fairness in the pattern of dismissing, the student must use random criteria, such as dismissing by birthday month or by the number of siblings or the types of pets families have.

Mediators support autonomy

Most of us use mediators to help us fulfill obligations: we set alarms, write notes to ourselves, and have people remind us of appointments. Similarly, the cleanup song, the call and response, and the timer help children know what to do and when to do it, without the teacher telling them. The mediators guide them closer to accomplishing tasks on their own instead of having to rely on the teacher for assistance.

Here is another example of a useful mediator: eventually, a young child will remember that s/he sits between Alicia and Bradley in the circle. Until then, s/he can look for his or her nametag on the floor in the circle, at the right spot, and feel the satisfaction of succeeding without being told what to do. Children embrace mediators largely because they fulfill their needs for autonomy and competence.

"Mediators function as scaffolding, helping children make the transition from maximum-assisted performance to independent performance...As children internalize mediators introduced by an adult, they are able to maintain the same high level of performance independently that was initially assisted by the adult."[3]

Other-regulation

What about children who don't pay attention? "If someone forgets or is not paying attention, what can we do to help?" the teacher asks the class as they are planning the transition routines in September. "You can tell them," exclaims a child. Telling each other what to do comes naturally to children. In fact, children often learn self-regulation by first engaging in other-regulation, directing the behavior of someone else. Like most people, they can see other people's mistakes more clearly than their own.

"We can even say that when it comes to learning a new behavior, children can regulate this behavior in other people before they are capable of regulating it in themselves."[4]

Read more about other-regulation in Chapter One, page 21.

Rehearsals for management

Once the class has the schedule displayed and a schedule manager to move the indicator, and mediators and transition leaders for switching from one activity and/or location to another, they need to rehearse. Rehearsing with different people directing the transitions, we'll become familiar with our routines.

One way to practice is to time travel: *Let's pretend that time is moving faster than usual, and in just one hour we can go through our whole day—how we will move from one activity to another, from arriving in the morning till we are ready to leave.*

Another way is to rehearse the transition right before you do it. For a few days, when it's time to change activities, stop five minutes early, rehearse the transition, and then do it, each part of the process led by a different student. When a procedure isn't very complicated and the children will probably do it well right away, try it out, then reflect and discuss: How well did we do? What part could we do better? Then try it again.

Elementary Designs practices develop self-regulation in classroom and school communities that aim to meet the fundamental needs of students. It is productive and respectful to ask children to suppress urges in a community where their needs are understood, respected, and met, and where they are given plenty of opportunities to express themselves, to be heard, and to lead. Read more about self-regulation in Chapter One, page 20.

Anticipating and Problem-solving Breakdowns

By now, we have established and found ways to support shared responsibility for routines. But every day is different, and there are many variables to deal with. Be prepared! Tell everyone: *Somebody will make a mistake, or we might be running late, or someone isn't cooperating. What will we do if things go wrong? Let's plan ahead how we will fix breakdowns.*

Breakdown

We forget to watch the clock, and we go past the transition time. **RESPONSE:** Children brainstorm solutions that might prevent forgetting next time, such as putting one person in charge of watching the clock.

Breakdown

Some students don't pay attention when transition time is signaled, or they want to finish one more thing. Others get impatient. **RESPONSE:** Children brainstorm solutions: someone can remind dawdlers; everyone else can go ahead; a student can walk around the classroom with a sign that says and shows what to do next: "Clean up," "Come to circle," "Line up," etc.

Our room helper held up a sign with a number on it indicating which round [rotation through centers] we were about to do next. She also had a "clean up" sign. I immediately noticed kids moving more slowly, more deliberately. And it was quiet—something I had not anticipated! (Second grade teacher)

Breakdown

Everyone cooperates in our transitions, but they take too long **RESPONSE:** Set a timer and record how long it takes, and try to better the time. Monitors can put away materials and/or collect trash. When someone finishes cleaning up, s/he can help someone else.

Today, after taking three deep breaths, I waited…took out my stopwatch and started it…waited…4 minutes and 33 seconds later, finally we were all silently seated on the rug and ready. At the next transition, we did the same thing, except this time the "inspector" silently walked around with a sign that said "Clean Up." This time the transition took 3 minutes and 25 seconds. It works! It will take patience on my part. The timer is a great tool. They began supporting each other and saying they wanted to beat their time. (Third grade teacher)

Breakdown

When we have to transition to music class, the children lag along in the hallway and are noisy. **RESPONSE:** Make a game of the transition:

I challenged the children to get to the music room without anyone knowing we were in the hall, and to surprise even the music teacher by moving silently into the room and getting into a circle. I tipped off the music teacher ahead of time, and she pretended to be busy at her desk while the children tiptoed in, circled up, and reveled in their "trick." The music teacher looked up in great surprise to find them there! Ever since then, this is their goal when transitioning to music: "Let's sneak in again!" They do the transition quickly and quietly. (First grade teacher)

Breakdown

Before the end of the work period, children start walking around and talking to each other instead of working right up to the transition. **RESPONSE:** Sometimes people get tired of sitting still and working. We could set up options for what to do when you need a break from sitting, such as stretches or standing or deep breathing exercises so you can refocus.

In my fifth grade room, we decided that a student could call for a "brain break." That meant we would all stop work, stand, and do a fun movement activity such as Jigalo or The Clown Got Sick or sing a song with gestures, such as "Threw It Out the Window." The rule was we had to work for at least seven minutes, but usually kids called for the breaks after about twenty minutes. Of course we reflected on how we were doing and reminded ourselves that if kids started overusing the brain break, we'd have to give it up. They got the idea, and it was never overused—just a booster when they needed one to keep working productively. (Fifth grade teacher)

Reflecting on How We Are Doing

Now it's time for the class to take stock. In a community circle, we think about how well our solutions are handling the breakdowns, and we look at the flow of the day and make sure it's going well. Partners can brainstorm ideas for improving either the schedule or how we handle the schedule, and we can choose the best ideas. Each of us can assess the job we're doing as leaders and as followers, and make plans for improvements.

- Do we have too many transitions? Could we get by with fewer?
- Can we improve leadership of the transitions?
- Do we want to change some of our music cues?
- Is there a way transitions could be more fun?
- Are we each making sure we are ready for the next thing?

We could assign a couple of students each day to be "checkers," to decide when everyone is ready for the transitions or ready to begin community circle or ready to go outside. We could invent visual mediators that would remind everyone to clean up or listen carefully or gather or return materials. The flow of our day is everybody's business, and everybody can help us get the most learning and fun out of our time together.

Aim for and celebrate student self-management

Today I told my students they've made a lot of progress since the beginning of the year in getting quiet, tracking the speaker, putting down whatever's in their hands, and so on, when a signal is given. Now that they all know what the various signals mean (hand up, chime, bump-ba-da-bump-bump, clap), I will simply start speaking when they have quieted down. It'll be up to them to do the rest...I'm hoping this will lead to the development of good habits with less teacher hand-holding. (Fifth grade teacher)

It's important for everyone's morale that we note our successes, but how we recognize them is important. Do not praise someone for doing a "good job," because this shifts the emphasis from the student's self-management to the teacher's approval. Occasional expressions such as:

"Wow—ready already?!" or

"We are getting really good at this transition stuff!" or

"We got ready so efficiently, we have five minutes before lunch. Let's play a game!"

Show your enthusiasm for students' competence and autonomy in managing themselves, without the condescension or manipulation of teacher praise.

At the end of the day, we can encourage the group to reflect on how the transitions went, and together review when there were bumpy waves and when there was smooth sailing. We can think about how well students managed themselves, and note whether teacher intervention was necessary at times. The goal is competence with self-regulation, not merely good teacher-directed transitions.

By encouraging partnership between adults and children for an orderly day, we create a more peaceful, less authoritarian, more self-regulated and collaborative classroom climate. We establish a culture that supports a willing embrace of order, and we reduce the likelihood that children will disrupt. The feeling is: "This is my classroom. I help make it a good place to be. I'm not going to mess it up, and I don't want anyone else to mess it up."

Observations support teacher-student attunement

Increased student ownership of the rhythms of the day provides children the chance to lead and to see that the teacher respects their ability to manage well without constant direction. While a student leads a transition, the teacher has an opportunity to observe and listen carefully:

I'm watching Michael try to do his job just right (making a mental note to tell him what I saw), and I'm observing the responses of the other children. I see that Claudia has a hard time quieting down, Latitia whispers the whole time, and Samuel always wants to be first. I see Carlo's frustration with what he has been working on, and Cecilia's untamed urge to tell others what to do.

Each piece of information gives me more insight into these learners. I'll jot down a couple of my observations and put them with the materials I'll use when I work one-to-one with the children. Then I can honestly say, "I've noticed that you ...."

"...children need to be seen...They need the encouragement and validation that comes from our best attention to their efforts. They need the safety that comes from the belief that their teacher sees them, knows them. Mutual trust grows from this security. When all children feel seen, they are released to work."[5]

The best way to truly "see" the learners in our care is to know and attune ourselves to them and to their families, to observe and listen to students carefully, to work with them individually and in groups in an atmosphere that is friendly, reciprocal, and playful enough so that everyone feels free to participate authentically. In such a culturally and personally inclusive climate, where all voices are heard, we can know our students as their authentic selves. Then, within the parameters of the curriculum, children can learn in ways that are best for them, with peer partners who help them think, with enough self-direction opportunities to feel respected and independent, and with the help of a teacher who guides them from success to success. One factor that enables the teacher to give her students what they need each day is getting what *she* needs from her colleagues, with whom she has trusting and mutually supportive relationships.

Orchestrating for Pro-social Behavior

Children who have chances to guide the behavior of others tend to manage their own behavior well at the same time. In fact, young children learn self-regulation best by first regulating the behavior of others. They know the rules, but it is when *others* break them that they can see the discrepancy between rule and behavior. Having children take turns directing the class through routines and transitions builds the consciousness as well as the experience of self-regulation.

In addition, because much misbehavior in the classroom involves children using their voices when they shouldn't, or being louder than is acceptable, providing more opportunities for them to talk—to a partner, to the group, to the whole class—helps satisfy the desire to have a voice in school, to express themselves, and to be heard.

Persistent disruption

Even when routines are generally going well, a few children might disrupt with behaviors that seem intended for attention-getting or rebellion or are the actions of a child who is unable to self-regulate. The teacher may impose loss of the privilege of being with the group (the child takes a break for a short time in a designated spot) or loss of the privilege of using certain equipment or engaging in an activity. Such consequences are usually characterized as "logical."

Even so, they may not work. The most important thing about redirecting a child successfully is that we know him well enough to be confident that the correction will calm him and allow him to regain his self-management. Understandably, it might be useful to have a child who has reached his limit of sitting do some more sitting in a time-out chair, rather than a few stretches or a more active, hands-on learning activity. And it may be counterproductive to withdraw the privilege of using scissors after an argument about who gets to use them, since the issue is not using the scissors appropriately, but the children's ability to negotiate sharing. Social, not mechanical, skills are lacking; the arguers need to rehearse and master taking turns. Until they do so, arguments will continue to occur over anything that needs to be shared. In short, the teacher must get to the root of the problem to address it effectively.

When I was in second grade, I had a lot of timeouts because I couldn't sit still and be quiet as much as we had to. After a while I didn't care. I'd rather get up and go to the time-out chair than keep sitting and sitting! (Ten year old girl)

Once we understand a child who repeatedly breaks the rules— once we see things, just for a moment, the way s/he does—we can structure our responses so they help the child develop self-controls.

Jimmy was a joker. He made silly wisecracks and faces, played jokes, purposely stumbled and fell, always to the merriment of classmates. One day I had him stay after school. We began to talk, and Jimmy said something silly, and in spite of myself, I laughed. I enjoyed him, just as his classmates did. He meant no harm; it just was very hard for him to resist a chance to make others laugh. Timing is everything, I told him, and he had to get a better feel for when a joke was appropriate, and when it would disrupt class. After that conversation, he disrupted class far less frequently, and when I looked at him with my serious eyes, he stopped. (Fifth/sixth grade teacher)

Backup

Every teacher must be able to get backup from the school crisis response team or from the office if a student's behavior is badly out of control. Often, however, the classroom is basically in control, but one or more children are disrupting. Think about what could be adjusted so they would find it easier to stick to the guidelines and routines. You might want to pause for a few minutes of movement (perhaps even go outside), try a mindfulness activity, give students some choices about the learning activity at hand, and/or add variety to activities. Remember the power of play to set things right when they seem to be going wrong!

Once order has been restored, reflect on root causes, and take steps to reduce the likelihood of the disruption occurring again.

Reflection and First Steps

How can I give students more leadership roles in transitions?

How can I involve students in addressing breakdowns in the rhythm of our day?

What mediators for routines do I want to try?

You could start by placing your current daily schedule next to a possible revision of the schedule. Then even if there seems to be little room for change, you could still consider incorporating one or two ideas or strategies from this book into the day. Highlight one idea that is an intention for tomorrow, next week, or next year.

1   Aydin Bal, Kathleen King Thorius, and Elizabeth Kozleski, "Culturally Responsive Positive Behavioral Support Matters," *The Equity Alliance at Arizona State University* (2012): 8, www.equityallianceatasu.org.

2   Tools of the Mind, "Self-Regulation," http://www.toolsofthemind.org/philosophy/self-regulation/.

3   Elena Bodrova and Deborah J. Leon, *Tools of the Mind: Vygotskian Approach to Early Childhood Education* (Upper Saddle River, NJ: Pearson, 2007), 57.

4   Ibid., 82.

5   Ruth Charney, *Teaching Children to Care* (Turners Falls, MA: Northeast Foundation for Children, 2002), 29.

CHAPTER SIX

Resources

KEY ASPECTS OF RELATIONAL TRUST IN SCHOOLS

From *Trust in Schools: A Core Resource for Improvement*, Anthony S. Bryk and Barbara Schneider

"*Respect*   In the context of schooling, respect involves recognition of the important role each person plays in a child's education and the mutual dependencies that exist among various parties involved in this activity. **Key in this regard is how conversation takes place within a school community. A genuine sense of listening to what each person has to say marks the basis for meaningful social interaction.**" (emphasis added, page 23)

Competence   In the school setting this refers to how others measure the value of a teacher's or principal's or staff member's job performance or contribution to the school community. This does not refer, in this case, to formal supervisory relationships, but to more informal observations or recognitions that are always being made in the school setting, both positively and negatively. (from pages 23-25)

"*Personal Regard for Others*   Any actions taken by a member of a role set (i.e. paraprofessionals, for example, or special education teachers) to reduce others' sense of vulnerability affects their interpersonal trust...When school community members sense being cared about, they experience a social affiliation of personal meaning and value. Such actions invite reciprocation from others and thereby intensify the relational ties between them. (page 25)

"*Integrity*   In a basic sense, we think of individuals as having integrity if there is consistency between what they say and do. ...integrity demands resolutions that reaffirm the primary principles of the institution. In the context of schooling, when all is said and done, actions must be understood as about advancing the best interests of children. Teachers demonstrate such integrity to their colleagues when they willingly experiment with new forms of instruction to improve student learning, even though this entails additional work and the risk of failure can be high. Similarly, principals do the same thing when they are willing to speak out, for example, against a central office policy they believe will not help the children. Behaviors of this sort publicly affirm an individual's commitment to the core purposes of the school community." (pages 25-26)

Anthony S. Bryk and Barbara Schneider, *Trust in Schools: A Core Resource for Improvement* (New York: Russell Sage Foundation, 2002).

- Poverty and "race" are closely connected in the United States. In 2007, 18% of American children lived in poverty, but 34% of African-American children, 33% of American Indian/Alaskan Native children, and 27% of Hispanic children did. At the same time, 10% of European-American children lived in poverty, and 11% of Asian-American children.

- High-school graduation rates in 2007 were on average 74%; 91% of Asian Americans graduated and 80% of European Americans. Hispanic, American Indian, and African-American students' graduation rates that year were 62%, 61%, and 60% respectively.

- The average percentage of students retained one grade level or more in 2007 was 11%, but 21% of African-American students were held back, compared to 9% of white students and 3% of Asian-American students.

- 43% of African-American students were suspended at least once in 2007, as were 22% of Hispanic students, compared to 16% of European-American students and 11% of Asian-American students.

- Only 1% of European-American students were expelled from school in 2007, compared to 13% African-American students.

- 5% European-American students and 21% of Hispanic students dropped out of school in 2007.

Students' achievement scores went down in proportion to the rate of all of these indicators. On the *National Assessment of Educational Progress* mathematics test results in 2009, European Americans and Asian/Pacific Islanders were the top scorers with 73 and 68% of them respectively scoring at or above the Basic level. Only 44% of Hispanics, 43% of American Indians/Alaskan Natives, and 38% of African-American adolescents achieved the Basic level.

Susan Aud, Mary Ann Fox, Angelina KewalRamani, "Status and Trends in the Education of Racial and Ethnic Minorities," National Center for Education Statistics (NCES) (July 2010) http://nces.ed.gov/pubs2010/2010015.pdf.

THEORY OF BASIC HUMAN NEEDS IN *ELEMENTARY DESIGNS* PRACTICES

Four basic needs of elementary-age children are addressed with *Elementary Designs* practices, helping them become proficient learners: strong, authentic relationships among students, between teachers and students, and among adults; personalized learning that ensures students' incremental and steady progress; opportunities to be heard, to lead, and to learn from each other, not just from a teacher. These practices address each child's need for:

- relationship with adults and peers
- a sense of their own competence
- the experience of autonomy
- the chance to play or find pleasure in learning

Children are motivated by their desire to satisfy these needs, and in the process of satisfying them, they develop socially and cognitively.

In the mid- to late 20th Century, psychologists explored and described what motivates people. Abraham Maslow[1] noted that people are motivated to satisfy their needs. In 1998, William Glasser presented his theory about how people's choices[2] are influenced by their needs for belonging, power, freedom, and fun. Earlier, psychiatrist and educator Rudolf Dreikurs explored how the needs to feel significant and to feel that we belong shape our behavior. He viewed the learner as a social being who learns by working collaboratively with peers.[3] And Erik Erikson's theory of development[4] said that human needs for relational trust, autonomy, and competence shape the way we develop our identity.

Lev Vygotsky, the father of cultural-historical psychology, described the ways social interactions shape people's language and cognitive growth, particularly through observing and interacting with one another.[5] Developmental psychologist Jean Piaget's work introduced the understanding that learning is an active, not passive, process, based on children's being given the autonomy to explore and discover.[6] And contemporary educator and psychologist Barbara Rogoff builds on Vygotsky and Piaget's work, viewing cognitive growth as generated by an "apprenticeship" in which a master guides the novice, steadily expanding the novice's understanding.[7]

Before Piaget's work, philosopher, psychologist, and educational reformer John Dewey[8] stressed the importance of students' active participation in their learning, creating as well as implementing the structures by which they live and work together in the classroom.

1 Abraham Maslow, *Motivation and Personality* (New York: Harper, 1954).
2 William Glasser, *Choice Theory* (New York: HarperCollins, 1998).
3 Rudolf Dreikurs, F.C. Peepers, & B.B. Grunwald, *Maintaining Sanity in the Classroom: Classroom Management Techniques* (New York: Taylor & Francis, 1998).
4 Erik Erikson, *Identity: Youth and Crisis* (New York: Norton, 1968).
5 Leo S. Vygotsky, *Thought and Language* (Cambridge: MIT Press, 1986). Original work published 1934.
6 Jean Piaget, *To Understand Is to Invent: The Future of Education* (New York: Grossman Publishers, 1973). [tr. of *Ou va l'education* (1971) and *Le droit a l'education dans le monde actuel* (1948)]
7 Barbara Rogoff, *Apprenticeship in Thinking: Cognitive Development in Social Context* (Oxford, England: Oxford University Press,1990).
8 John Dewey, Democracy and Education: An Introduction to the Philosophy of Education (New York: Macmillan, 1916).

BEYOND THE BAKE SALE FAMILY PARTNERSHIP RESOURCE

The following resource is an excerpt from *Beyond the Bake Sale: The Essential Guide to Family-School Partnerships*, pages 15-18, reprinted with permission.[1] Review the four sets of descriptions, pages 166-170, under the qualities of family-school engagement: Building Relationships; Linking to Learning; Addressing Differences; Supporting Advocacy; Sharing Power. Consider which best describe the interaction in your school and where you might focus your energy to better partner with families.

Partnership School

All families and communities have something great to offer— we do whatever it takes to work closely together to make sure every single student succeeds.

❑ BUILDING RELATIONSHIPS

- Family center is always open, full of interesting learning materials to borrow
- Home visits are made to every new family
- Activities honor families' contributions
- Building is open to community use and social services are available to families

❑ LINKING TO LEARNING

- All family activities connect to what students are learning
- Parents and teachers look at student work and test results together
- Community groups offer tutoring and homework programs at the school
- Students' work goes home every week, with a scoring guide

1   *Beyond the Bake Sale: The Essential Guide to Family-School Partnerships*-Copyright © (2007) by Anne T. Henderson, Karen L. Mapp, Vivian R. Johnson, and Don Davies. Reprinted by permission of The New Press. www.thenewpress.com

❑ ADDRESSING DIFFERENCES

- Translators are readily available
- Teachers use books and materials about families' cultures
- PTA includes all families
- Local groups help staff teach parents

❑ SUPPORTING ADVOCACY

- There is a clear, open process for resolving problems
- Teachers contact families each month to discuss student progress
- Student-led parent-teacher conferences are held three times a year for thirty minutes

❑ SHARING POWER

- Parents and teachers research issues such as prejudice and tracking
- Parent group is focused on improving student achievement
- Families are involved in all major decisions
- Parents can use the school's phone, copier, fax, and computers
- Staff work with local organizers to improve the school and neighborhood

Open-Door School

Parents can be involved at our school in many ways—we're working hard to get an even bigger turnout for our activities. When we ask the community to help, people often respond.

❑ **BUILDING RELATIONSHIPS**
- Teachers contact families once a year
- Parent coordinator is available if families have questions or need help
- Office staff are friendly
- Staff contact community agencies and organizations when help is needed

❑ **LINKING TO LEARNING**
- Teachers explain test scores if asked
- Folders of student work go home occasionally
- School holds curriculum nights three or four times a year
- Staff let families know about out-of-school classes in the community

❑ **ADDRESSING DIFFERENCES**
- Office staff will find a translator if parents ask in advance
- Multicultural nights are held once a year
- "Minority" parents have their own group

❑ **SUPPORTING ADVOCACY**
- Principal will meet with parents to discuss a problem
- Regular progress reports go to parents, but test data can be hard to understand
- Parent-teacher conferences are held twice a year

❑ **SHARING POWER**
- Parents can raise issues at PTA meetings or see the principal
- Parent group sets its own agenda and raises money for the school
- Resource center for low-income families is housed in a portable classroom next to the school
- PTA officers can use the school office
- A community representative sits on the school council

Come-if-We-Call School

Parents are welcome when we ask them, but there's only so much they can offer. The most important thing they can do is help their kids at home. We know where to get help in the community if we need it.

❑ **BUILDING RELATIONSHIPS**

- Better-educated parents are more involved
- "Many immigrant parents don't have time to come or contribute"
- Staff are very selective about who comes into the school

❑ **LINKING TO LEARNING**

- Parents are told what students will be learning at the fall open house
- Parents can call the office to get teacher-recorded messages about homework
- Workshops are offered on parenting

❑ **ADDRESSING DIFFERENCES**

- "We can't deal with twenty different languages"
- "Parents can bring a translator with them"
- "The school isn't the same as it used to be"

❑ **SUPPORTING ADVOCACY**

- School calls families when children have problems
- Families visit school on report card pickup day and can see a teacher if they call first

❑ **SHARING POWER**

- Principal sets agenda for parent meetings
- PTA gets the school's message out
- "Parents are not experts in education"
- Community groups can address the school board if they have concerns

Fortress School

Parents belong at home, not at school. If students don't do well, it's because their families don't give them enough support. We're already doing all we can. Our school is an oasis in a troubled community. We want to keep it that way.

❑ BUILDING RELATIONSHIPS

- Families do not "bother" school staff
- "Minority families don't value education"
- Parents need security clearance to come in
- It is important to keep community influences out of the school

❑ LINKING TO LEARNING

- Curriculum and standards are considered too complex for parents to understand
- "If parents want more information, they can ask for it"
- "We're teachers, not social workers"

❑ ADDRESSING DIFFERENCES

- "Those parents need to learn English"
- "We teach about our country—that's what those parents need to know"
- "The neighborhood is going downhill"

❑ SUPPORTING ADVOCACY

- Parents don't come to conferences
- Problems are dealt with by the professional staff
- Teachers don't feel safe with parents

❑ SHARING POWER

- Principal picks a small group of "cooperative parents" to help out
- Families are afraid to complain: "They might take it out on my kid"
- "Community groups should mind their own business; they don't know about education"

STUDENT PROFILE

Name:

Assets profile:

Developmental profile:

Preferred learning mode:

Personal/cultural profile:

Needs profile:

What could I do and say to support his/her growth?

WHOLE-GROUP LESSON WITH A PROJECT-BASED FOLLOW UP

The following example uses the E4 format for follow-up projects introduced in Chapter Three, page 96. A class of third graders in an urban school studied immigration to the United States.

Exploration

First, the whole group created a timeline of the history of immigration to the United States, including numbers of people, where they came from, their contributions, their struggles for human rights, and the influence of wars.

...the sorting [of events] took only a few days and was totally student-run. They had an extremely high interest level in the project. I could see that my role during this project...[was to be] a guide and facilitator. What struck me most was once the timeline was complete (it covered the whole blackboard of the classroom with maps included) they had an organic conversation that I witnessed about how they were surprised by when things happened in history, especially regarding inventions, wars, and human rights. They were questioning each other, making "I notice" statements. I said nothing, just listened...They used the timeline as a reference throughout their six-week project.

Next, students listened to two read-alouds: *Coming to America: The Story of Immigration* and *The Keeping Quilt.* With a world map handy for reference, they read about Ellis Island independently and in groups and simulated immigrant arrivals there, learning vocabulary such as "green card," "refugee," and "asylum."

I modeled putting text in your own words. We did a simulation activity called "Nacirema," [adapted to fit this age group] about what it feels like to be an outsider. This was extremely powerful for them, and they wrote reflections about the experience.

In the second week of the project, the class did more read-alouds: *Dreaming of America: An Ellis Island Story; I Was Dreaming to Come to America: Memories from Ellis Island Oral History Project;* and *Watch the Stars Come Out.* Students took a test of their map skills on a United States map, and they continued using world maps.

In Week Three they prepared to interview immigrants. After generating lists of questions, they wrote letters to four adults in the school community who were immigrants, each from a different country: India, Somalia, Vietnam, and Russia. Students were divided into four groups, one for each immigrant. They began independent reading of leveled books of historical fiction, and they discussed the genre. The new read-alouds were *How Many Days to America?*; *How My Family Lives in America*; and *I Hate English!*

Expression

During the Week Three explorations, students worked with the art teacher to make images that reflected immigrants' experiences. In Week Four, they conducted the interviews and began to process the information they collected. And there was another read-aloud: *In the Year of the Boar and Jackie Robinson.*

Exhibition and evaluation

In Week Five, students transformed their interviews into Power-Point presentations to families and to other classes. They created a museum that included the timeline, exhibits the students made, and their art images. They created a guide that included a map of the museum, explanations of the exhibits, and reviews of the books they had read during the unit. The exhibition was a rewarding climax, and anticipation of it was an impetus throughout the unit.

During the unit, each session ended with a group reflection in the circle or with partners sharing with each other what they had accomplished during the work period that day.

This obviously helped them stay focused and accountable. It was also a great gauge for me to learn where they were in the process. I think they learned a lot from each other during these reflections, hearing about others' work and process or progress.

At the conclusion of their projects, students reflected in writing about the unit as a whole, in a free write and in response to specific, focused questions or a rubric.

Thank you, Katie Haag, for sharing this teaching experience with us.

PROJECT PLAN

Task

	Quality work includes: ☐ ☐ ☐
?	Questions
	Observations/research
	Plan
	First try
	Partner talk
	Teacher talk
	Ready for my audience
✓	How did I do? Check off quality work list above.

DAILY SCHEDULE

TIME	TASK	✓
8:30	Hello! Morning challenge with partner	
9:00	First circle of the day	
9:30	Reading: choices or centers and work with Ms. A.	
10:50	Community circle: work share	
11:00	Community circle: science/social studies	
11:45	Recess and lunch	
12:30	Math: varied activities or centers and work with Ms. A	
1:35	Community circle: work share	
1:45	Music	
2:45	Community circle: work share or read- aloud or other quick whole-class learning	

SHARING STUDENTS' GROWTH WITH THEIR FAMILIES

See the example below of a Yes! card that can be sent home with students to recognize moments of growth. There is no formula for their design. They can be about the size of index cards, big enough to contain a specific, positive comment about social or academic skills gained. Student illustrations can add to the spirit of celebration.

LITERACY GROWTH RECORD-KEEPING EXAMPLES

Here are examples from one teacher's record of reading growth. Students use one form throughout the year to circle the sound blends the student can read proficiently, and check and re-check later in the semester, in case proficiency has slipped (see Word Work example below). Every week, the teacher listens to each child read, noting any issues and/or reading tips s/he gives the student, and records a sign of growth, then compliments the child on that growth (see Reading Record below). S/he monitors each child's writing to make sure they spell the sound combinations correctly. In this way, s/he is able to monitor students' incremental successes in reading weekly. S/he may use a reading test three times per year as a more comprehensive marker. The goal, as always in personalized learning, is that each child progresses at his or her personalized rate and knows s/he is progressing incrementally and steadily.

Thank you, Kirsten Holmquist, for sharing your record-keeping examples with us.

Reading Record

Date:	# of completed stories [student has read]
Title: [stories/books read]	
Notes: [benchmark skills worked on in session]	
Compliment:	
Tip: [what to work on]	

Word Work: First grader at end of year

Students circle the phonemes as they demonstrate proficiency in reading them.

My la

e, u, i, sh, th,

dr, tr, a-e, o-e,

ai, i-e, ea, oa,

igh, ew, aw, or,

ou, oi, ir

endings:
ed, es, ies,
pping, ding

Students circle the phonemes as they demonstrate proficiency in reading them.

Ethan

ai , i-e, a-e, oa,

igh, ew, aw,

ou, ir, (tr)

endings:

ed, es, ies,

pping, ding

PARTNER REFLECTION FORM

Name: _____

Who did you help? _____

How did you help them? (check all that apply)
- ☐ I reminded my partner to keep working
- ☐ I watched my partner work (check for accuracy)
- ☐ I listened to my partner read his or her words

Here's how I encouraged them (compliment):

_____

RHYTHM PLAY FOR COMMUNITY CIRCLES

Begin the meeting with rhythm play, an activity that bonds and energizes the group. Children walk in a circle rhythmically, counting aloud "one-two-three-four." The first time around the circle, everyone emphasizes the first beat vocally and with a louder footfall; on the second round, the second beat, and so on.

Instead of marching, you can pass a clap around the circle, emphasizing numbers as above. Initially, everyone counts aloud as the claps go around the circle. When this is mastered, they can try keeping the rhythm smooth using only the claps, eliminating counting aloud. This activity can be done with different rhythms, such as two claps for each number or using combinations of steps and claps. Best of all, invite the children to make up rhythms. You can be sure their rhythms will present greater complexity and will push everyone to go faster!

VARIATION: start a clapping rhythm (or have a child start one) that everyone joins in, then the leader changes the rhythm and the group adopts the new rhythms.

Rhythm play teaches children:

- to focus their attention
- to regulate themselves so they clap only at the right times and in the right way
- to remember and use the right rhythm at the right time

HOW I FEEL WHEN I'M LEFT OUT

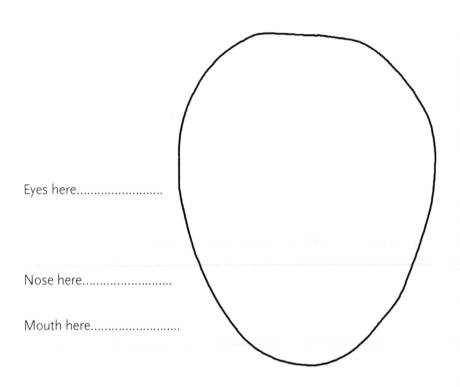

Eyes here...........................

Nose here...........................

Mouth here...........................

Compare the feeling you have when you're left out with something else that feels sad or uncomfortable.

For example:

- When I'm left out I feel like I'm in a cold, wet rain when I'm wearing only a t-shirt.

- When I'm left out I feel like a dog left alone when everyone leaves the house.

When I'm left out I feel like: _____

_____

_____

_____

_____

_____

ACTIVITIES FOR THE POWER OF PLAY

Here are examples of the three categories of fun activities: quick, funny, and active.

Quick fun: Zoom

Everyone sits in a circle, and the person who begins the activity says "Zoom," turning her/his head quickly to a neighbor on either the right or the left as s/he says it. That person passes the "zoom" to the next person, and so on, around the circle. The idea is for the circle to move the "zoom" as fast as they can. To challenge the group to go faster, use a stopwatch, and keep a record of the class's times.

When they have mastered the game, you can add challenge by adding "Eeek!" (a screeching halt) as a possibility. When someone says "Eeek," the "zoom" suddenly reverses direction. At first, allow just one eek per round; later, increase the permitted number of eeks.

Funny fun: Pass the Mask

Give students a moment to think up a silly facial expression. One player starts by making a face, then turns to his/her neighbor. The neighbor mimics the face, then turns to the next person and makes the facial expression s/he devised. A variation is to pass a silly sound instead of a face. The result of either is lots of laughter.

Active fun: Kitty Wants a Corner

One person is Kitty. S/he walks around the inside of the circle, stops, and says to a student, "Kitty wants a corner," and the student responds, "Ask my neighbor." While this is happening, any student can make eye contact with another, exchange nods (an agreement to switch seats), and then the two try to trade seats before Kitty can get to one of their chairs and sit down. The object for Kitty is to take someone's seat, and the person left standing becomes Kitty. Because more than one pair can switch seats at the same time, there is a lot of action in this game. Rehearse safe chair-changing before play begins (stop the game if children begin to crash into one another). Because the game requires careful observation and body control, it is excellent for cultivating self-regulation in children.

Active fun: The Clown Got Sick

This is a simple call and response which keeps everyone active. Repeat the following group chant and action sequence around the circle.

Student: "The clown got sick."
Group: "How did the clown get sick?"
Student: "The clown got sick by doing this." (does an action with arms, legs, and/or whole body)
Group: "The clown got sick by doing this!" (group repeats the action)

All players continue the action until the next person says, "The clown got sick," and a new action is introduced. Rehearse a few actions before you begin the activity, then challenge students to invent their own and not repeat a previous action. Give them a moment to think up a motion before you begin.

Selected Bibliography

We list here the main texts used when writing this book. See endnotes for complete references.

Anrig, Greg. *Beyond the Education Wars: Evidence that Collaboration Builds Effective Schools.* New York: The Century Foundation Press, 2013, Kindle edition.

Ashton-Warner, Sylvia. *Teacher.* New York: Simon & Schuster, 1963.

Banks, James A. *Educating Citizens in a Multicultural Society.* 2nd ed. New York: Teachers College Press, 2007.

Bodrova, Elena and Deborah J. Leong. *Tools of the Mind: The Vygotskian Approach to Early Childhood Education.* 2nd ed. Upper Saddle River, NJ: Pearson, 2007.

Brown, Stuart and Christopher Vaughan. *Play: How it Shapes the Brain, Opens the Imagination, and Invigorates the Soul.* New York: Avery, 2009.

Bryk, Anthony S. and Barbara Schneider. *Trust in Schools: A Core Resource for Improvement.* New York: Russell Sage Foundation, 2002.

Bryk, Anthony S. et al. *Organizing Schools for Improvement: Lessons from Chicago.* Chicago: University of Chicago Press, 2010.

Capps, Donald. *The Decades of Life: A Guide to Development.* Louisville: Westminster John Knox Press, 2008.

Carter, Prudence L. and Kevin G. Weiner, eds. *Closing the Opportunity Gap: What America Must Do to Give Every Child an Even Chance.* New York: Oxford University Press, 2013.

Charney, R., Clayton, M., Lord, J., Wood, C. *A Notebook for Teachers: Making Changes in the Elementary Curriculum.* 1985. rev. ed. Greenfield, MA: Northeast Foundation for Children, 1993.

Crawford, Linda. *Face to Face Advisories: Bridging Cultural Gaps in Grades 5-9.* Minneapolis: The Origins Program, 2013.

———. *Lively Learning: Using the Arts to Teach the K-8 Curriculum.* Turners Falls, MA: Northeast Foundation for Children, 2004.

Darling-Hammond, Linda. *The Flat World and Education: How America's Commitment to Equity Will Determine Our Future.* New York: Teachers College Press, 2010.

Delpit, Lisa. *"Multiplication is for White People": Raising Expectations for Other People's Children.* New York: The New Press, 2013.

———. *Other People's Children: Cultural Conflict in the Classroom.* New York: The New Press, 1995.

Dineen, Margo Holden. *If They Can Do It, We Can Too! Kids Write about Famous People Who Overcame Learning Differences Similar to Theirs.* Minneapolis: Fairview Press, 1992.

Duckworth, Eleanor. *"The Having of Wonderful Ideas" and Other Essays on Teaching and Learning*. New York: Teachers College Press, 2006.

Dweck, Carol. *Mindset: The New Psychology of Success: How We Can Learn to Fulfill our Potential*, New York: Ballantine, 2008.

Ellison II, Gregory C. *Cut Dead But Still Alive: Caring for African American Young Men*. Nashville: Abington Press, 2013.

Estes, Eleanor. *The Hundred Dresses*. New York: Harcourt, 1944.

Fox, Jennifer. *Your Child's Strengths: A Guide for Teachers and Parents*. New York: Penguin Books, 2008.

Fredrickson, Barbara L. *Positivity*. New York: Three Rivers Press, 2009.

Goleman, Daniel. *Focus: The Hidden Driver of Excellence*. New York: HarperCollins, 2013.

Gorski, Paul C. *Reaching and Teaching Students in Poverty: Strategies for Erasing the Opportunity Gap*. New York: Teachers College Press, 2013.

Hartmann, Thom. *The Edison Gene: ADHD and the Gift of the Hunter Child*. Rochester, VT: Park Street Press, 2003.

Heaney, Seamus. *Poems 1965-1975: Death of a Naturalist / Door Into the Dark / Wintering Out / North*. New York: Farrar and Strauss, 1966.

Henderson, Anne T., Karen L. Mapp, Vivian R. Johnson, and Don Davies. *Beyond the Bake Sale: The Essential Guide to Family-School Partnerships*. New York: The New Press, 2007.

Jones, Charlotte. *Mistakes that Worked: 40 Familiar Inventions and How They Came to Be*. New York: Delacourt Press, 1991.

Kahn, Salman. *The One World Schoolhouse: Education Reimagined*. London: Grand Central Publishing, 2012.

Katz, Bob. *Elaine's Circle: A Teacher, a Student, a Classroom, and One Unforgettable Year*. New York: Marlowe and Company, 2005.

Kirp, David. *Improbable Scholars: The Rebirth of a Great American School System and a Strategy for America's Schools*. New York: Oxford University Press, 2013.

Landsman, Julie. *Growing Up White: A Veteran Teacher Reflects on Racism*. Lanham, MD: Rowman and Littlefield Education, 2008.

Martin, Jr., Bill and John Archambault. *Knots on a Counting Rope*. New York: Henry Holt & Co., 1987.

Muhammad, Anthony and Sharroky Hollie. *The Will to Lead, the Skill to Teach: Transforming Schools at Every Level*. Bloomington, IN: Solution Tree, 2012.

Newberg, Andrew and Mark Robert Waldman. *Words Can Change Your Brain: 12 Conversation Strategies to Build Trust, Resolve Conflict, and Increase Intimacy*. New York: Plume, 2013.

Nieto, Sonia and Patty Bode. *Affirming Diversity: The Sociopolitical Context of Multicultural Education*. 6th ed. Boston: Pearson, 2012.

Orfield, Gary and Erica Frankenberg and Associates *Educational Delusions? Why Choice Can Deepen Inequality and How to Make Schools Fair*. Berkeley: University of California Press, 2013.

Palmer, Parker J. *The Courage to Teach: Exploring The Inner Landscape of A Teacher's Life*. San Francisco: Jossey-Bass, 1998.

_____. *A Hidden Wholeness: The Journey Toward an Undivided Life*. San Francisco: Jossey-Bass, 2004.

Perry, Theresa, Robert P. Moses, Joan T. Wynne, Ernesto Cortes, Jr. and Lisa Delpit, eds. *Quality Education as a Constitutional Right*. Boston: Beacon Press, 2010.

Post, Thomas. "The Role of Manipulative Materials in the Learning of Mathematical Concepts," *Selected Issues in Mathematics Education*. Berkeley: McCutchan Publishing, 1981.

Pransis, Kay. *The Little Book of Circle Processes: A New/Old Approach to Peacemaking*. Intercourse, PA: Good Books, 2005.

Rogoff, Barbara. *Apprenticeship in Thinking: Cognitive Development in Social Context*. New York: Oxford University Press, 1990.

Sahlberg, Pasi. *Finnish Lessons: What Can the World Learn from Educational Change in Finland?* New York: Teachers College Press, 2011.

Sharroky, Hollie. *Culturally and Linguistically Responsive Teaching and Learning*. Huntington Beach, CA: Shell Education, 2012.

Siegel, Daniel J. *Pocket Guide to Interpersonal Neurobiology: An Integrative Handbook of the Mind*. New York: W.W. Norton, 2012.

Stevens, Luc, Wim van Werkhoven, Jos Castelijns. *The Attunement Strategy: Reclaiming Children's Motivation by Responsive Education*. Geneva: International Bureau of Education, 2001.

Tough, Paul. *How Children Succeed: Grit, Curiosity, and the Hidden Power of Character*. Boston: Houghton Mifflin, 2012.

Vygotsky, L.S. "Thinking and Speech." In *The Collected Works of L.S. Vygotsky, Volume 1: Problems of General Psychology*, edited by R.W. Rieber and A.S. Carton. New York: Plenum Press, 1987.

Wigfield, Alan and Jacquelynne S. Eccles. *The Development of Achievement Motivation*. San Diego: Academic Press, 2002.

Wood, Chip. *Time to Teach, Time to Learn: Changing the Pace of School*. Greenfield, MA: Northeast Foundation for Children, 1999.

_____. *Yardsticks: Children in the Classroom, Ages 4-14*. 3rd ed. Turners Falls, MA: Northeast Foundation for Children, 2007.

Wood, Chip and Babs Freeman-Loftis. *Responsive School Discipline: Essentials for Elementary School Leaders*. Turners Falls, MA: Northeast Foundation for Children, 2011.

Warren, Mark R., Karen Mapp, and The Community Organizing and School Reform Project. *A Match On Dry Grass: Community Organizing as a Catalyst for School Reform*. New York: Oxford University Press, 2011.

Zweirs, Jeff and Marie Crawford. *Academic Conversations: Classroom Talk That Fosters Critical Thinking and Content Understandings*. Portland, ME: Stenhouse, 2011.

Linda Crawford and Chip Wood

About the Authors

CHIP WOOD, M.S.W., is an educator whose career has included community organizing; working in schools as a teacher, a principal, a parent educator, and a district administrator; and serving as executive director of an educational non-profit. He is the Inaugural Fellow at The Origins Program in Minneapolis, Minnesota, focusing on issues of equity in education. He is co-developer of the *Elementary Designs* approaches outlined in this book. He has been a facilitator for the Center for Courage & Renewal for the past 18 years, offering reflective professional development experiences for teachers and school leaders based on the work of Parker J. Palmer. He is a co-developer and facilitator for *Leading Together: Building the Adult Community of Schools.* In 1981, Chip co-founded Northeast Foundation for Children and was a co-developer of the *Responsive Classroom* approach to elementary school teaching. He is the author of *Yardsticks: Children in the Classroom Ages 4-14* (2007); *Time to Teach, Time to Learn: Changing the Pace of School* (1999) and co-author of *Responsive School Discipline* (2011). Chip and his family live in Buckland, Massachusetts.

LINDA CRAWFORD founded The Origins Program and is now Lead Program Developer there. She has taught kindergarten through graduate school, and she was principal of an arts-integrated elementary school for five years. She has led professional-development seminars and workshops for educators for over thirty years. She is co-developer of the *Elementary Designs* approaches outlined in this book and the *Developmental Designs* approach to integrated social and academic learning for adolescents. She is the author of *Face to Face Advisories: Bridging Cultural Gaps in Grades 5-9* (2013); *Classroom Discipline: Guiding Adolescents to Responsible Independence* (co-author, 2009); *The Advisory Book: Building a Community of Learners Grades 5-9* (2008); *Lively Learning: Using the Arts to Teach the K-8 Curriculum* (2004); and *To Hold Us Together: Seven Conversations for Multicultural Understanding* (1990). She has produced videos on multicultural education through the arts and has published numerous articles on the integration of social and academic learning. She has a BS in English Education from the University of Wisconsin and an MA in English Literature from the University of Minnesota. She lives with her family in Minneapolis.

The Origins Program and *Elementary Designs*™ Approaches

The Origins Program, a nonprofit educational organization, is the home of the *Elementary Designs* and *Developmental Designs* (grades 5-9) approaches. Since 1979, thousands of educators have participated in Origins workshops, consulting, and book-study groups, and *Developmental Designs* publications are in use in hundreds of middle schools.

The Origins Program's mission is to promote an equitable and humane multicultural society through quality education for all. Its vision is every young person eager and able to contribute to the peace, prosperity, and wellness of the world.

Elementary Designs developers Linda Crawford and Chip Wood have worked for decades to build equity education. Their work is founded on research and tested in classrooms. Their core beliefs include that learning must integrate curriculum content and home cultures; that it must empower all students to learn through constructing their own understanding, to learn by expressing themselves in a variety of modes, and to learn in a school environment that is safe, playful, and authentic.

Learn more through an *Elementary Designs* three-day workshop

The workshop includes time to plan implementation of *Elementary Designs* practices, to work with a partner to deepen learning, to engage in daily practices to remain centered, to examine resources for honing students' skills during independent practice, and to use community meetings and management strategies that empower students to express themselves positively and lead their peers.

Crawford and Wood understand and appreciate the challenges of daily school life. They meet educators exactly where they are, and help them grow step by step, from success to success, so that they can meet the needs of all students. They have designed a workshop that invites educators to partner with colleagues, to pick a starting place and move toward what they have always wanted: **education for everyone, with no one left out.**

THE ORIGINS PROGRAM
EDUCATION FOR EQUITY

WORKSHOPS | CONSULTING | RESOURCES
www.originsonline.org | 800-543-8715 | 612-822-3422